HOW THE CIA KILLED CHE

"Sorting through the archives of the fallen Arbenz regime in Guatemala City a few weeks after the [1954] coup, [CIA official] David Atlee Phillips came across a single sheet of paper about a twenty-five-year-old Argentine physician who had arrived in town the previous January to study medical care amid social revolution. 'Should we start a file on this one?' his assistant asked. The young doctor, it seemed, had tried to organize a last-ditch resistance by Arbenz loyalists; then he sought refuge in the Argentine Embassy, eventually moving on to Mexico. 'I guess we'd better have a file on him,' Phillips replied. Over the coming years the file for Ernesto Guevara, known as 'Che,' became one of the thickest in the CIA's global records."

Gentleman Spy: The Life of Allen Dulles by Peter Grosse

HOW THE CIA KILLED CHE
THE MURDER OF A REVOLUTIONARY

MICHAEL RATNER AND MICHAEL STEVEN SMITH

Skyhorse Publishing

Published by arrangement with OR Books, New York. © 2011 by Michael Ratner
and Michael Steven Smith
Preface © 2016 by Michael Ratner and Michael Steven Smith
Introduction © 2016 by Greg Grandin

First Skyhorse Publishing edition 2016

This book was previously published by OR Books as *Who Killed Che?:
How the CIA Got Away with Murder*

Skyhorse Publishing books may be purchased in bulk at special discounts for
sales promotion, corporate gifts, fund-raising, or educational purposes. Special
editions can also be created to specifications. For details, contact the Special Sales
Department, Skyhorse Publishing, 307 West 36th Street, 11th Floor, New York,
NY 10018 or info@skyhorsepublishing.com.

Skyhorse® and Skyhorse Publishing® are registered trademarks of Skyhorse Publishing,
Inc.®, a Delaware corporation.

Visit our website at www.skyhorsepublishing.com.

10 9 8 7 6 5 4 3 2 1

Library of Congress Cataloging-in-Publication Data is available on file.

Cover design by Rain Saukas
Cover photo credit AP Images

Print ISBN: 978-1-5107-1101-3

Printed in United States of America

DEDICATION

This book is dedicated to our friend, attorney Leonard Weinglass (1933-2011). For fifty-three years Len took on what he called "the machinery of the state," by defending extraordinarily courageous women and men fighting for social justice against the American imperium. He died representing the Cuban Five, Cuban patriots jailed for their efforts to prevent counter-revolutionaries based in Miami from launching terrorist attacks against people and property in Havana.

Len will be remembered: personally, for his good company, wide-ranging intellect, generous spirit, loyalty, kindness and gentleness; politically, as an excellent persuasive speaker, an acute analyst of the political scene and a far-seeing visionary who understood that capitalism was not compatible with democracy; and professionally, as one of the great lawyers of his time, joining the legal pantheon of leading twentieth-century advocates for justice.

Leonard Weinglass: Presente!

ANOTHER DEDICATION

Michael Ratner (1943–2016) was my dearest friend and a collaborator in various ways on six books, especially this one, which only came about because of the initiative he took in making a FOIA request that yielded two boxes of documents from the US government. When he died on May 11, 2016 we lost one of the great lawyers of his generation.

—Michael Steven Smith

CONTENTS

Praise for *How the CIA Killed Che*

"Ratner and Smith cut through the lies and distortions to provide a riveting and thoroughly documented history of the murder of Che Guevara."
—Amy Goodman, host of *Democracy Now!*

"Michael Ratner and Michael Smith, relying on newly disclosed government documents, have exposed what many of us who worked as reporters in Latin America long suspected—the CIA ordered the assassination of the revolutionary leader Ernesto 'Che' Guevera after he was captured in Bolivia. This is not surprising. The CIA had tried to assassinate Guevara, along with Fidel Castro, before. Once Guevara was in the hands of Bolivian military units, which were accompanied by a CIA operative named Felix Rodriguez, the CIA got its chance. A Bolivian soldier may have pulled the trigger. The Bolivian government may have been blamed. But the execution order, Ratner and Smith demonstrate, came directly from Washington. This is one more crime, among the many crimes of empire, Washington has attempted to hide. Now it cannot."
—Chris Hedges, Pulitzer-prize winning reporter for the *New York Times* and author of *War is a Force That Gives Us Meaning*

"A page-turner with meticulous research that burrows deep into the archives of recently declassified documents to tell the full story of how Che Guevara was hunted and killed."
— Jane Franklin, historian and author of *Cuba and the U.S. Empire*

"With formal US-Cuba ties restored, Smith and Ratner have provided a great service of documentation. Washington's fear and hostility toward Cuban revolutionary and other Latin American leaders is amply shown in its effort to track down and assassinate Che Guevara, and then to try to cover up its responsibility in Che's killing. Readers everywhere will appreciate their contribution toward defeating historical amnesia."
—Walter Lippmann, Editor-in-Chief, CubaNews Yahoo News Group

"Nowadays, the US government relies on drones to hit and kill generic as well as specific 'targets'—be they, flora, fauna, military equipment or economic and natural resources. The scorched earth approach is not new in US foreign and even domestic policy. This book clearly shows the specific, efficient machinery of assassination that targeted one man—Ernesto Che Guevara.

The assassins were Cuban Americans and Bolivian soldiers in the employ of the US government and the CIA in particular. This was the most famous of their victims but not the only one. Assassination as a weapon of foreign policy did not start nor end with the murder of Ernesto Guevara. As the authors note, 'Che's death was critical to the U.S., to ensure that the example of the Cuban revolution would not inspire other revolutionary movements.'

Yet, in death, Che continued to be an inspiration. This book is well researched and insightful and while relying on the canons of academic research, it is also a thorough, intellectual left critique of US policy. As important is the portrayal and discussion of Ernesto Guevara Serna—Che—as a unique man and revolutionary. If Che were still alive, he would recognize that the US government has turned a significant portion of the world into many Vietnams."

—Nelson P Valdés, Professor Emeritus, University of New Mexico

"Mincing no words, Michael Ratner and Michael Smith deliver a stinging indictment of a government hell-bent on silencing an extraordinary humanitarian leader. This eye-opening gem of a book—with riveting original source materials—is a must read for all seeking the truth behind Che Guevara's assassination."

—Heidi Boghosian, co-host of *Law and Disorder*

Preface

The republication of our book is timely and welcome. Five years ago we told the story of how and why the American government, through the Central Intelligence Agency, assassinated Cuban revolutionary leader Che Guevara in the town of La Huegara, Bolivia on October 9, 1967. It was a war crime. Che had been taken prisoner and was executed. Sadly, US assassination practices have continued, whether by drone or by soldiers from JSOC, the Joint Special Operation Command. Assassinations by the US are not likely to end.

One big change in the years since our last publication was President Obama's recognition that American policy of isolation and aggression against Cuba had been a failure. On March 22, 2016 in front of an eight-story high metal portrait of Che Guevara in Havana's Plaza of the Revolution, Obama made a promise saying that "Cuba's destiny will not be decided by the United States or any other nation. Cuba is sovereign and rightly has great pride. The future of Cuba will be decided by Cubans, not by anybody else." We are sure Obama is speaking falsely. Yes, part of the blockade has been eased and diplomatic relations opened. But it's very one sided. Cuba can buy from the United States but cannot sell most of its products to the United States. Nonetheless it's a major victory after over fifty years of a severe embargo which cost the Cubans over $100 billion and stunted the development of their economy.

Che's assassination was a blow to Cuba's internationalism and support for international movements. It was a blow, but not a fatal one, as Cuba continued to support revolutions in Central and South America as well as liberation movements in Africa. The US did not want what occurred in Cuba to happen elsewhere. Cuba's popular revolution had committed the "crime" of taking over their own economy by nationalizing vast American property holdings, installing the 99% in power, and seeing the 1% flee to Miami. The US had initially been successful in isolating Cuba. The governments of Brazil, Bolivia, Argentina, Uruguay and Chile were overthrown for not going along with this American policy. An economic, commercial, and financial blockade of the island was started. President Dwight D Eisenhower, pursuant to a 1960 memo written by a senior state department official, initiated "a line of action that makes the greatest inroads in denying money and supplies to Cuba, to decrease monetary and real wages, to bring about hunger, desperation and the overthrow of the (Castro) government."

Che Guevara conceived of, helped organize, and led a band of international guerrilla fighters in Bolivia whose mission was to defend the Cuban revolution by extending it first to Bolivia and then to Argentina and ultimately throughout Latin America. This ended with his murder.

But eventually America itself had become isolated. At the 2014 Summit of the Americas conference the United States was told by the countries of the Caribbean and Latin America that either Cuba be allowed to attend the next conference or America need not come. Popular opinion throughout the US and even in Florida had changed. American commercial interests in agribusiness, travel, and pharmaceuticals pressed the government to change its policy. It did. After 56 years, Obama declared an end to much of the last vestige of the Cold War, although not completely. There is still more to do. Since then travel restrictions to Cuba by Americans have been lightened, although tourism is still outlawed. The financial, economic, and commercial blockade of Cuba has been partly lifted but this still has a long way to go. The Helms-Burton law which makes regime change in Cuba the policy of the American government is still on the books and can only be reversed through an act of Congress. America still funds programs to recruit Cubans and subvert the Cuban government. The public reversal of American policy would not have happened but for the steadfastness and support the Cuban people have manifested in the more than a half a century since they made their revolution.

But is America's changed policy an attempt by other means to do what it has been trying to do since the Cuban social revolution of 1959, mainly to reverse it and reestablish capitalist property relations on the island? Will the United States continue to propagandize against Cuba with the charge that it is a human rights violator? Will its commercial efforts succeed in establishing class divisions, setting Cubans against each other, undermining their solidarity, and undermining the socialist institutions that the Cuban people have created to advance their common good? We do not have a crystal ball but we do know the nature of American imperialism.

Che embodied the hope of succeeding generations that the world can and must be changed. That hope has now been partially accomplished with the recognition of Cuba and the steps taken towards the normalization of relations. It is our hope that our book will help put this recognition into its historical context and help foster solidarity with the Cuban people.

"Viva Che"

Michael Ratner
Michael Steven Smith
New York City, April 2016

FOREWORD

KILLING CHE: THE HIDDEN HAND

"Everyone must be prepared to swear that he has not heard of it."
—President Dwight D. Eisenhower

This book presents a perceptive and coherent explanation of the death of Ernesto Che Guevara, on October 9th 1967, after he had been captured, injured, and disarmed two days previously. Attorneys Ratner and Smith demonstrate, with numerous declassified documents and irrefutable arguments, that: "the U.S. Government, particularly its Central Intelligence Agency, had Che murdered, having secured the participation of its Bolivian client state."

It was not just a run-of-the-mill crime. It was one for which a state was responsible, and the burden of guilt evidently falls on people who held the highest government posts in Washington. Ratner and Smith set out the magnitude of the crime: "Under the laws that govern warfare, including guerilla war, the killing of a prisoner is murder and constitutes a war crime. It is not the actual shooter who is guilty of a war crime. Those higher up that ordered, acquiesced or failed to prevent the murder are guilty of a war crime as well. There is no statute of limitation for this crime."

Recognizing that Che's guerilla movement was the most serious threat to their plans for hemispheric domination, the U.S. government held defeating Che and his comrades as its highest priority. That its representatives murdered him, using the intermediaries of Bolivian soldiers, is something that should not surprise anyone. After all, official violence, including torture and death, practiced by regimes imposed by the United States—who trained, armed and advised the torturers and murderers—was by no means rare in those days, or now for that matter. Rather it strikes us as curious, to say the least, how some have accepted and disseminated the official American version of the story that the U.S. government was not responsible for Che's death.

In the 60s, the United States strived to isolate the Cuban Revolution, and openly pressed Latin American governments to yield to its anti-Cuban strategy. A few resisted. Among them, only Mexico was capable of maintaining diplomatic relations with Cuba and surviving. The others—Brazil, Bolivia, Argentina,

Uruguay and Chile—were to pay an extremely high price for their dissent. One after the other, starting in 1964 with the overthrow of President Goulart of Brazil and President Paz Estensoro of Bolivia, these countries suffered the dissolution of their democratic institutions and their replacement with the worst of tyrannies, entirely supported by successive U.S. governments. Tens of thousands of Brazilians, Bolivians, Argentineans, Uruguayans, Chileans and other Latin Americans died at the hands of local henchmen, trained and guided by American advisors. Today, many still remain on the dreadful lists of the "disappeared."

Ernesto Guevara was an object of interest for the American secret services before he entered our history, long before he became 'Che.' The United States, in particular, worked tirelessly to do away with the guerillas in Bolivia. To that end, they openly intervened in the country, not only by training and equipping the local military, but also by placing American officials and agents in positions of command.

This was not the first time Washington had done this, nor the first time they had tried to kill Che and his comrades. During the Cuban guerilla war against Batista's dictatorship, the Eisenhower Administration implemented the same approach as that later applied by the Johnson Administration in Bolivia.

At the end of 1956, Fidel Castro, with a group of revolutionaries including Che, disembarked on the east of the island to create a guerilla movement against the Batista dictatorship. They suffered significant setbacks in the first weeks after their arrival. Batista's propaganda machine—and the American media—announced the liquidation of the guerillas and even Fidel's death.

The truth, hidden from the public, was moving in another direction altogether, something the Eisenhower Administration understood. The administration went to great pains to arm and prepare Batista's troops to combat the guerillas. In 1991, the State Department partially declassified—with the usual crossing-outs and omissions—a set of hitherto-secret documents relating to Cuba (Foreign Relations of the United States. 1958-1960 Volume VI Cuba).

The documents reveal the extent of the American participation in the early stages of the conflict. They describe how "200 men of MAP[US Military Assistance Program]-supported[1] battalion (First Battalion, First Infantry Regiment) of Cuban Army was transferred to Oriente Province a few days after landing there

---

1 U.S. Military Assistance Program

on December 2, 1956 of group led by Fidel Castro . . . In late May 1957 entire battalion of approximately 800 men moved to Oriente and is still there. From 75 to 90 percent of its officers have received MAP training." And it was not only the infantry that received instruction from the US: "approximately 70 percent of all officers of Cuban Air Force have received MAP training."[2]

Also evident was the American involvement in the Batista dictatorship's machinery of repression set up under the Police, the Bureau of Investigations, the Bureau for the Repression of Communist Activities (BRAC), the Military Intelligence Service, and the Naval Intelligence Service. The officers in these organizations had studied in American academies, and American advisors were stationed in their headquarters.

As the crisis of the Cuban dictatorship intensified, concern rose in Washington. On Christmas Eve 1958, in a dramatic meeting at the White House, the Head of the CIA asserted that "we ought to prevent a Castro victory," and the Secretary of State, summarizing the discussion, observed that "opinion as to the undesirability of a Castro regime appeared to be unanimous." A couple of days later, Eisenhower indicated that "he did not wish the specifics of covert operations to be presented to the NSC."

These efforts, of course, failed and the struggle of the people of Cuba against Batista's dictatorship was successful. The United States then intensified its covert operations, launching an economic war, military aggression, and terrorist violence against Cuba. In all of this activity it attempted to adhere to Eisenhower's guideline that: "our hand should not show in anything that is done."

Among the many ways that the American empire has used to preserve its dominance, suppression and manipulation of information stands out. The essence of this is to conceal or falsify the truth and spread the lie. Michael Ratner and the Center for Constitutional Rights have carried out a consistent battle against such untruths and secrecy. This book serves as an additional proof of its co-editors' determination to defend truth, adherence to the law, and freedom.

As the book itself does, I would like to finish with some thoughts on Che's legacy. The American empire may have had him murdered in cold blood, with premeditation and cowardice, but it did not succeed in killing him. Today Che

---

2 Telegram From the Embassy in Cuba to the Department of State Havana, February 7,1958. (http://www.latinamericanstudies.org/cable/cable-2-7-58.htm)

is more alive than ever. He lives on through his image, worn on the chests of millions around the world. He has become a standard bearer for all those who want a better world and are prepared to fight to get it. Che remains alive, above all, in a Latin America that today is building a new politics of independence and solidarity, a politics that owes a great deal to his ideals and his sacrifice.

His spirit also lives on through the lives of the Cuban Five: Gerardo, Ramón, Antonio, Fernando and René, who have been unjustly imprisoned for more than twelve years for fighting anti-Cuban terrorism sponsored by Washington. When they were kids, they had promised they would be like him. In their prisons, subjected to cruel treatment, in utter solitude, our five heroes testify that Che is still with us today.

Ricardo Alarcón de Quesada,
President of the Cuban National Assembly, 1993–2013

Introduction

There he was, Che Guevara, hovering over Barack Obama in Havana's Plaza de la Revolución, during the U.S. president's state visit to the island in March 2016, as part of the rapprochement between Cuba and the United States currently underway. The Argentine-born Cuban revolutionary, killed in 1967 in Bolivia at the behest of Washington, as Michael Ratner and Michael Smith here show, looked down implacably on the official proceedings like the Angel of History, or maybe, despite his face not carrying even a hint of a smile, some cosmic Cheshire Cat.

Years ago, the great New Left filmmaker Chris Marker made a documentary on the global political tumult of the 1960s and 1970s, of which Che was a player and, after his execution, an icon. The English version of the film was titled "A Grin without a Cat," a reference to the famous feline character in *Alice in Wonderland*, which appears and disappears at will, leaving behind only his grin. The title was a critique of the post–Cuban Revolution insurrectionary New Left, which abandoned not only the stultifying conservatism of Soviet Communism but also Communism's political base. Guerilla movements, especially in Latin America, both inspired by Che (in Argentina, Venezuela, Guatemala, and Mexico, among other places) and led by Che (in Bolivia), met with catastrophe. In Marker's words, would-be insurgents made themselves into "a spearhead without a spear, a grin without a cat." More broadly, Marker's title alluded to the gap between the hope of global socialism (the grin) and its failure (the missing cat). But the promise has outlived the particular politics of its moment. After all, in Carroll's *Alice in Wonderland*, the Cat survives the Queen of Heart's death sentence, since one "couldn't cut off a head unless there was a body to cut it off from."

Many didn't survive of course. After the triumph of the Cuban Revolution in 1959, Washington sponsored, instructed, and funded death-squad regimes throughout the hemisphere, in Chile, Argentina, Uruguay, Brazil, Bolivia, Colombia, El Salvador, Nicaragua, Guatemala, Honduras, among other countries, killing or disappearing hundreds of thousands of people and torturing hundreds of thousands more. But the ideal of the New Left wasn't vanquished. It returned with strength in the early part of this century, propelling to power one left and center-left government after another—in Brazil, Venezuela, Ecuador, Argentina, and Bolivia. These governments and the social movements that supported them were forced to operate on a vastly different terrain, largely accepting the validity and constraints of the electoral system yet remaining faithful to an unabashedly left agenda of solidarity, equality, and liberty.

Che, too, returned, despite the post–Cold War effort to turn him into a caricature of a bloodthirsty revolutionary terrorist, not unlike the Queen of Hearts, "shouting 'Off with his head!' or 'Off with her head!' about once in a minute." This depiction never took hold in Latin America, even among those who are hostile to the politics he represents. For the many millions of Latin Americans who do share his ideals, Che remains the grin, a promise of living a life committed to something other than the marketplace, of morals that aren't ruthlessly commodified, and of affective ties that aren't merely transactional. I remember living in Guatemala in the early 1990s, as its civil war was winding down and it became possible to say things in public that had once been prohibited. Suddenly there appeared, among the laminates of the Virgin Mary and Janet Jackson hawked by vendors on the streets, Che t-shirts. Guevara, who justified shutting down civil society in Cuba based on his experience of watching the CIA destabilize civil society in Guatemala in 1954, was here an icon of free speech.

There are other ironies. If we believe Fidel Castro's account, it was he who—having in the 1960s sponsored insurgencies throughout Latin America—advised activists such as Evo Morales to resist the lure of armed revolution and engage fully with electoral politics. Morales, of course, went on to become one of the most successful presidents in Bolivian history, in the process rehabilitating, celebrating, and memorializing Che, who died on Bolivian soil trying to launch a guerrilla revolt. "Why do I like Che?" Evo Morales, repeating a journalist's question, "I like Che because he fought for equality, for justice," Morales told me. "He did not just care for ordinary people; he made their struggle his own."

Greg Grandin,
Brooklyn, New York

CHRONOLOGY

CHE GUEVARA AND THE CUBAN REVOLUTION

June 14, 1928
Ernesto Guevara is born in Rosario, Argentina, of parents Ernesto Guevara Lynch and Celia de la Serna.

1945-51
Guevara is enrolled at medical school in Buenos Aires.

January-July 1952
Guevara visits Peru, Colombia, and Venezuela. While in Peru he works in a leper colony treating patients.

March 10, 1952
Fulgencio Batista carries out coup d'état in Cuba.

March 1953
Guevara graduates as a doctor.

July 6, 1953
After graduating, Guevara travels throughout Latin America. He visits Bolivia, observing the impact of the 1952 revolution.

July 26, 1953
Fidel Castro leads an armed attack on the Moncada army garrison in Santiago de Cuba, launching the revolutionary struggle to overthrow the Batista regime. The attack fails and Batista's troops massacre more than 50 captured combatants. Castro and other survivors are soon captured and imprisoned.

December 1953
Guevara has first contact with a group of survivors of the Moncada attack in San José, Costa Rica.

December 24, 1953
Guevara arrives in Guatemala, then under the elected government of Jacobo Arbenz.

January 4, 1954
Guevara meets Ñico López, a veteran of the Moncada attack, in Guatemala City.

January-June 1954
Unable to find a medical position in Guatemala, Guevara obtains various odd jobs. He studies Marxism and becomes involved in political activities, meeting exiled Cuban revolutionaries.

June 17, 1954
Mercenary forces backed by the CIA invade Guatemala. Guevara volunteers to fight.

June 27, 1954
Arbenz resigns.

September 21, 1954
Guevara arrives in Mexico City after fleeing Guatemala.

May 15, 1955
Fidel Castro and other Moncada survivors are freed from prison in Cuba due to a massive public campaign in defense of their civil rights.

June 1955
Guevara encounters Ñico López, who is also in Mexico City. Several days later, López arranges a meeting for him with Raúl Castro.

July 7, 1955
Fidel Castro arrives in Mexico with the goal of organizing an armed expedition to Cuba.

July 1955
Guevara meets Fidel Castro and immediately enrolls as the third confirmed member of the future guerilla expedition. Guevara subsequently becomes

involved in training combatants, with the Cubans giving him the nickname "Che," an Argentine term of greeting.

November 25, 1956

Eighty-two combatants, including Guevara as doctor, sail for Cuba aboard the small cabin cruiser *Granma*, leaving from Tuxpan in Mexico.

December 2, 1956

Granma reaches Cuba at Las Cooradas beach in Oriente Province. The rebel combatants are surprised by Batista's troops and dispersed. A majority of the guerillas are either murdered or captured; Guevara is wounded.

December 21, 1956

Guevara's group reunites with Fidel Castro; at this point there are 15 fighters in the Rebel Army.

January 17, 1957

Rebel Army overruns an army outpost in the battle of La Plata.

May 27-28, 1957

Battle of El Uvero takes place in the Sierra Maestra, with a major victory for the Rebel Army as it captures a well-fortified army garrison.

July 1957

Rebel Army organizes a second column. Guevara is selected to lead it and is promoted to the rank of commander.

May 24, 1958

Batista launches an all-out military offensive against the Rebel Army in the Sierra Maestra. The offensive eventually fails.

August 31, 1958

Guevara leads an invasion column from the Sierra Maestra toward Las Villas Province in central Cuba, and days later signs the Pedrero Pact with the March 13 Revolutionary Directorate, which has a strong guerilla base there. Several days earlier Camilo Cienfuegos had been ordered to lead another column toward Pinar del Río Province on the western end of Cuba.

October 16, 1958
The Rebel Army column led by Guevara arrives in the Escambray Mountains.

December 1958
Rebel columns including Guevara and the March 13 Revolutionary Directorate and Cienfuegos with a small guerilla troop of the Popular Socialist Party, capture a number of towns in Las Villas Province and effectively cut the island in half.

December 28, 1958
Guevara's column begins the battle of Santa Clara, the capital of Las Villas.

January 1, 1959
Batista flees Cuba. A military junta takes over. Fidel Castro opposes the new junta and calls for the revolutionary struggle to continue. Santa Clara falls to the Rebel Army. Guevara and Cienfuegos are ordered immediately to Havana.

January 2, 1959
Cuban workers respond to Fidel Castro's call for a general strike and the country is paralyzed. The Rebel Army columns of Guevara and Cienfuegos arrive in Havana.

January 8, 1959
Fidel Castro arrives in Havana, greeted by hundreds of thousands of people.

February 9, 1959
Guevara is declared a Cuban citizen in recognition of his contribution to Cuba's liberation.

February 16, 1959
Fidel Castro becomes prime minister.

May 17, 1959
Proclamation of the first agrarian reform law, which fixed legal holdings at a maximum of 1,000 acres and distributed land to peasants.

October 7, 1959
Guevara is designated head of the Department of Industry of the National Institute of Agrarian Reform (INRA).

October 21, 1959

Following an attempt to initiate a counter-revolutionary uprising, Huber Matos, military commander of Camagüey Province, is arrested by Army Chief of Staff Camilo Cienfuegos.

October 28, 1959

Camilo Cienfuego's plane goes down over sea. Cienfuegos is lost at sea.

November 26, 1959

Guevara is appointed president of the National Bank of Cuba.

July-October 1960

Cuba nationalizes all major foreign and domestic industries and banks.

April 17-19, 1961

1,500 Cuban-born mercenaries, organized and backed by the United States, invade Cuba at the Bay of Pigs on the southern coast. The aim was to establish a "provisional government" to appeal for direct U.S. intervention. They are defeated within 72 hours, with the last fighters surrendering at Playa Girón, now the name used by the Cubans for the battle. Guevara is sent to command troops in Pinar del Río Province.

October 22, 1962

President Kennedy initiates the "Cuban Missile Crisis," denouncing Cuba's acquisition of missiles capable of carrying nuclear warheads for defense against U.S. attack. Washington imposes a naval blockade on Cuba. Cuba responds by mobilizing its population for defense. Guevara is assigned to lead forces in Pinar del Río Province in preparation for an imminent U.S. invasion.

October 28, 1962

Soviet Premier Khrushchev agrees to remove Soviet missiles in exchange for U.S. pledge not to invade Cuba.

March 1964

Guevara meets with Tamara Bunke (Tania) and discusses her mission to move to Bolivia in anticipation of a future guerilla expedition.

December 9, 1964

Guevara leaves Cuba on a three-month state visit, speaking at the United Nations. He then visits a number of African countries.

March 14, 1965

Guevara returns to Cuba and shortly afterwards drops from public view.

April 1, 1965

Guevara delivers a farewell letter to Fidel Castro. He subsequently leaves Cuba on an internationalist mission in the Congo, entering through Tanzania. Guevara operates under the name Tatú, Swahili for "number two."

April 18, 1965

In answer to questions about Guevara's whereabouts, Castro tells foreign reporters that Guevara "will always be where he is most useful to the revolution."

June 16, 1965

Castro announces Guevara's whereabouts will be revealed "when Commander Guevara wants it known."

October 3, 1965

Castro publicly reads Guevara's letter of farewell at a meeting to announce the Central Committee of the newly-formed Communist Party of Cuba.

December 1965

Castro arranges for Guevara to return to Cuba in secret. Guevara prepares for an expedition to Bolivia.

January 3-14, 1966

Tricontinental Conference of Solidarity of the Peoples of Asia, Africa, and Latin America is held in Havana.

March 1966

Arrival in Bolivia of the first Cuban combatants to begin advance preparations for a guerilla detachment.

July 1966

Guevara meets with Cuban volunteers selected for the mission to Bolivia at a training camp in Cuba's Pinar del Río Province.

November 4, 1966

Guevara arrives in Bolivia in disguise and using an assumed name.

November 7, 1966

Guevara arrives at site where Bolivian guerilla movement will be based; first entry in Bolivian diary.

November-December 1966

More guerilla combatants arrive and base camps are established.

December 31, 1966

Guevara meets with Bolivian Communist Party secretary Mario Monje. There is disagreement over perspectives for the planned guerilla expedition.

February 1-March 20, 1967

Guerilla detachment leaves the base camp to explore the region.

March 23, 1967

First guerilla military action takes place, with combatants successfully ambushing a Bolivian army column.

April 10, 1967

Guerilla column conducts a successful ambush of Bolivian troops.

April 16, 1967

Publication of Guevara's Message to the Tricontinental, including his call for the creation of "two, three, many Vietnams."

April 17, 1967

Guerilla detachment led by Joaquín is separated from the rest of the unit. The separation is supposed to last only three days but the two groups are unable to reunite.

April 20, 1967
Régis Debray is arrested after having spent several weeks with a guerilla unit. He is subsequently tried and sentenced to 30 years' imprisonment.

May 1967
U.S. Special Forces arrive in Bolivia to train counter-insurgency troops of the Bolivian Army.

July 6, 1967
Guerillas occupy the town of Sumaipata.

July 26, 1967
Guevara gives a speech to guerillas on the significance of the July 26, 1953 attack on the Moncada garrison.

July 31-August 10, 1967
Organization of Latin America Solidarity (OLAS) conference is held in Havana. The conference supports guerilla movements throughout Latin America. Che Guevara is elected honorary chair.

August 4, 1967
Deserter leads the Bolivian army to the guerillas' main supply cache; documents seized lead to arrest of key urban contacts.

August 31, 1967
Joaquín's detachment is ambushed and annihilated while crossing a river after an informer leads government troops to the site.

September 26, 1967
Guerillas walk into an ambush. Three are killed and government forces encircle the remaining guerilla forces.

October 8, 1967
Remaining 17 guerillas are trapped by Bolivian troops and conduct a desperate battle. Guevara is seriously wounded and captured.

October 9, 1967

Guevara and two other captured guerillas are murdered, following instructions from the Bolivian government and Washington.

October 15, 1967

In a television appearance Fidel Castro confirms news of Guevara's death and declares three days of official mourning in Cuba. October 8 is designated Day of the Heroic Guerilla.

October 18, 1967

Castro delivers memorial speech for Guevara in Havana's Revolution Plaza before an audience of almost one million people.

February 22, 1968

Three Cuban survivors cross border into Chile, after having traveled across the Andes on foot to elude Bolivian army. They later return to Cuba.

Mid-March 1968

Microfilm of Guevara's Bolivian diary arrives in Cuba.

July 1, 1968

Guevara's Bolivian diary published in Cuba is distributed free of charge to the Cuban people. The introduction is by "Fidel C."

CHE GUEVARA, HIS LIFE AND DEATH

"Mendacity is a system that we live in."
—Tennessee Williams, *Cat on a Hot Tin Roof*

Che Guevara has been dead for forty-four years. The history of who is responsible for his murder has heretofore not been understood accurately, especially in America, where it is commonly believed that the Bolivian military dictatorship had him killed. Documents which have recently been obtained from the U.S. government lead to a different conclusion: that the U.S. government, particularly its Central Intelligence Agency, had Che murdered, having secured the participation of its Bolivian client state.

On October 9, 1967, in the small rural village of La Higuera, Bolivia, at approximately 1:15 in the afternoon, a Bolivian army sergeant, Mario Teran, after fortifying himself with alcohol, walked into the mud-walled schoolhouse where Che, already wounded, was being held prisoner, and shot him dead. It was murder. Under the laws that govern warfare, including guerilla war, the killing of a prisoner is murder and constitutes a war crime. It is not just the actual shooter who is guilty of a war crime. Those higher-ups that ordered, acquiesced to, or failed to prevent the murder are guilty as well. There is no statute of limitations for this crime.

The initial story of Che's death, as presented by the Bolivians, was that he was killed in battle. Eventually it emerged that this was a lie and that he had, in fact, been taken prisoner and shot the next day. The Johnson administration claimed that the order to murder him came from the Bolivian high command and not the United States. It was further asserted that the United States, despite having a CIA operative at the scene disguised as a Bolivian military officer, was unable to prevent the murder.

This version of events insists that the United States was somehow opposed to the murder and wanted Che kept alive. Two days after the murder on October 11, 1967, Walt Whitman Rostow, President Lyndon Johnson's Special Assistant for National Security Affairs (the post now known as National Security Advisor), called the killing of Che "stupid," leaving the impression that somehow he and

Johnson were opposed to it [**Document 32, p146**] and that the CIA, under the control of the President, was not involved. Before looking in more detail at the circumstances surrounding Che's death and the CIA's relation to it, a brief examination of the modus operandi of the organization from its outset is useful.

The Creation of the CIA, its Autonomy, and the Practice of Plausible Deniability

The foundations of the American National Security State were laid with the National Security Act of 1947. The Act created the National Security Council and the CIA, granting the new intelligence agency particular powers that were, in the words of George Marshall, the Secretary of State at the time, "almost unlimited." Marshall warned President Truman of this before the Act was passed. Truman was later to agree with Marshall.[1]

In 1948 the National Security Council approved a secret directive, NSC 10/2, authorizing the CIA to carry out an array of covert operations including "propaganda, economic warfare, preventive direct action, sabotage, anti-sabotage, demolition and evacuation measures; subversion against hostile states including assistance to underground resistance movements, guerillas, and refugee liberation groups.[2]" This allowed for the CIA to become a paramilitary organization, a role that today is openly acknowledged as the Agency employs murderous drones flying assassination trips over Afghanistan and Pakistan. Before he died, George F. Kennan, the American diplomat and Cold War strategist who sponsored NSC 10/2 said that, in light of later history, it was "the greatest mistake I ever made.[3]"

Since NSC 10/2 authorized violations of international law it also established an official policy of lying so as to cover up the law-breaking. As James W. Douglas wrote, "The national security doctrine of "plausible deniability" combined lying with hypocrisy. It marked the creation of a Frankenstein monster.[4]" Plausible deniability encouraged the autonomy of the CIA and other covert-action ("intelligence") agencies from the government that created them. In order to protect the visible authorities of the government from protest and censure, the CIA was authorized not only to violate international law but to do so with as little consultation as possible. CIA autonomy went hand-in-glove with plausible deniability. The less explicit an order from the president, the better it was for "plausible deniability." And the less consultation there was, the more creative CIA authorities could become in interpreting the mind of the president . . .[5]

Richard Helms, the CIA's deputy director of planning in the 1960s, who had conspired to kill Castro, and who was to later head the agency, testified to the Church Committee in 1975 that "he never informed either the president or his newly appointed CIA director John McCone of the assassination plots." Nor did he inform any other official in the Kennedy administration. Helms said he "sought no approval for the murder attempts because assassination was not a subject that should be aired with higher authority.[6]" When he was asked if President Kennedy had been told, Helms said that "nobody wants to embarrass a President of the United States by discussing the assassination of foreign leaders in his presence.[7]"

The Written Record Relating to Che's Death

That the United States, and particularly the CIA, was not implicated in Che's murder, has been accepted by almost every writer on the subject, including those present in La Higuera. Even those sympathetic to Che accept, more or less, the account of Felix Rodriguez, the CIA operative who was present at Che's death, disguised as a Bolivian captain. He claims to have been the highest ranking officer on the scene at the time and to have relayed by radio the order from the Bolivian generals in La Paz to murder Che. In his book, *Shadow Warrior: the CIA Hero of a Hundred Unknown Battles,* he insists that he had been told by the CIA that if Che were captured alive he was to "do everything possible to keep him alive— everything![8]" Rodriguez says he could have countermanded the murder order and saved Che's life, but he chose not to, leaving Che's fate in the hands of the Bolivians[9]. This story makes little sense. Rodriguez was working for the CIA and would continue to do so for many years. If his bosses and paymasters wanted Che kept alive, he surely would have done so. If he had disobeyed the CIA's avowed wishes to "do everything" to keep Che alive, would he have been allowed to continue as a CIA operative? The obvious conclusion is the CIA wanted Che dead and that the story was crafted to give the White House "plausible deniability."

Jorge G. Castaneda, the Mexican writer, in his biography of Che, *Companero, The Life and Death of Che Guevara,* seems to accept Rodriguez's story that the

Americans wanted Che kept alive and that the order to murder him came from the Bolivians before "pressure . . . from the American's became intolerable.[10]" Castaneda tries to refute what he calls the "semiofficial Cuban version" of Che's death in which the President of Bolivia, Barrientos, visits the American ambassador and is told to kill Che[11]. To do so, Castaneda cites communications from Douglas Henderson, the U.S. Ambassador to Bolivia at the time, who says he was not consulted by the Bolivians about what to do with Che, and would have wanted him kept alive. While Castaneda admits Henderson could be covering up U.S. involvement in Che's murder, he says the Rostow October 11, 1967, memorandum to President Johnson calling the killing "stupid" supports non-U.S. involvement in the murder[12]. As is discussed below, the Rostow memorandum is undercut by its analysis of the benefits of Che's killing: if he knew in advance of plans to murder Che, adding the word "stupid" gives President Johnson plausible deniability. Alternatively, it is possible that the CIA was involved without the knowledge of Rostow, Henderson, or the President—though, because of the murder's major foreign policy implications, that scenario is unlikely.

To his credit, Castaneda does cite evidence that implicates the U.S. in the murder. He writes that U.S., or at least the head of the CIA country team in Bolivia, had a prior agreement or understanding with the Bolivians that Che would be killed if captured. According to Castaneda, Gustavo Villoldo, the head of the country team, told him in an interview that upon his arrival in Bolivia, he was driven to Barrientos's home to meet him. Villoldo told Barrientos in no uncertain terms that if Che were captured he personally would do everything in his power to have him executed. Then he asked, "If we take Che alive, what will you do with him"? The president replied: "If he is alive, he will be summarily judged and condemned to death. You have my word as the President of the Republic.[13]"

Jon Lee Anderson, in his popular biography *Che Guevara: A Revolutionary Life,* recounts Felix Rodriguez's story of relaying the death sentence from Bolivian generals in La Paz to the soldiers holding Che via his U.S.-government-supplied radio, and doing so despite the American government's purported desire to keep Che alive and interrogate him in Panama. Anderson provides a second version of the events, based on his examination of Bolivian Army Colonel Andres Selich's notes, shown to him by Selich's widow. Selich was on the scene at La Higuera at the time of Che's murder. Anderson writes that according to Selich, the Bolivian generals in La Paz sent Colonel Joaquin Zentano Anaya a radio message to kill Che. This meant it did not go to Rodriguez. Lt. Colonel Ayoroa, commander of the unit that captured Che, was to be responsible for the execution. While we do not know which, if any, of these stories are true, none exonerate the CIA or other American officials. Under any of the scenarios, as is demonstrated below, the CIA knew of Che's capture, and had its agent on the ground at the scene. Furthermore, the United States government had every reason to want Che dead. A revolution in Bolivia might have ignited revolutions in adjoining Andean countries, as Che has hoped and planned. The various stories merely attempt to put the CIA in the background with a story of plausible deniability.

Paco Ignacio Taibo II, a Mexican novelist and historian sympathetic to Che, authored the book *Guevara, Also Known as Che*. In it he recounts the transmission of the order to kill Che without mentioning any involvement of Rodriguez. He says that a message regarding Che's capture was sent on the evening of October 8 to the high command in La Paz. They then met with General Alfredo Ovando and General Juan Jose Torres, the army Chief of Staff, and may have consulted with other military officers. Taibo says there was no record of what was discussed in that room, only of the decision: Che Guevara had been sentenced to death. They then "consulted with President Barrientos.[14]" The implication in Taibo's account is that this group of generals and the President of Bolivia had made the decision to kill Che. However, from this account we do not know what, if any, input the U.S. and the CIA had in this decision. Taibo also appears to doubt Rodriguez's claim that he tried to convince the Bolivians not to kill Che. As Taibo observes, the Bolivian on the scene in La Higuera, Colonel Zenteno, who supposedly transmitted the order to kill Che, makes no mention of Rodriguez. In the end Taibo is forced to conclude that what occurred at La Higuera "is a morass of words that only leaves room for questions.[15]"

Fox Butterfield Ryan, a former State Department officer who taught at Georgetown University, has written the best-researched account of Che's murder in his 1998 book *The Fall of Che Guevara*. Like many, he admires Che for his valor and sacrifice, but not for his politics. He opposes the Cuban Revolution in general, and Fidel Castro in particular. Of all of these writers he is the closest to pinning the responsibility on the United States, although he concludes that "although it was deeply involved in eliminating Guevara's guerillas, it (the United States Government) neither killed nor ordered him to be executed."

Ryan acknowledges that there are many stories as to what happened, but he believes Che was executed on the orders of the President of Bolivia and the high command, not by the CIA. At the same time, he recognizes that there were many reasons the United States wanted Che dead and asks "[w]hy should an American Ambassador have saved Che Guevara?[16]" He points out that when the U.S. took the position of leaving Che's fate to the Bolivians, it had "no illusions" about what that would mean[17]. Although there is really no reliable, verifiable basis for Ryan stating that the U.S. was not involved in the order to execute Che, his conclusion is that the U.S. wanted him dead—they just did not want the visible blood on their hands. Ryan's story makes the U.S. at least morally, if not legally, culpable in Che's murder. By his account, the CIA knew for thirty-six hours before Che's execution that he was being held, but, he writes, "like Pontius Pilate," they did nothing.

The writer who appears to want most to exonerate the United States in Che's execution is Richard L. Harris, author of *Death of a Revolutionary*. Harris stands at the opposite end of the debate from Ryan, and his conclusion, that the CIA wanted Che kept alive, practically amounts to disinformation. Admitting that most of his sources are Bolivian, he concludes that the CIA was not responsible for Che's execution, that the CIA "appears" to have opposed his execution, that for "purely professional reasons" they wanted to keep him alive, and that "the U.S. contribution to the military defeat of Che's guerilla operation was minimal.[18]"

Contrary to most of these writers, the documentary evidence, which we present below, reveals that the U.S. did everything in its power "to eliminate the guerillas," including Che. [**Document 20, pp. 123-124**] The documents demonstrate that it was in the U.S. government's interest to have Che killed. The CIA and U.S. Special Forces trained the Bolivian Ranger Battalion that captured Che; CIA agents disguised as Bolivian officers accompanied the Rangers into the field; the U.S. supplied the weapons and provided the intelligence; and a CIA agent apparently was present at the time of his murder.

Moreover, the documentary evidence demonstrates that the American government and the CIA wanted Che dead even before he went to Bolivia. Che, of all the guerilla fighters of that period, exemplified the success of guerilla warfare against U.S. imperialism. His death was critical to the U.S., to ensure that the example of the Cuban revolution would not inspire other revolutionary movements.

CIA Attempts to Assassinate Che

Few of the writers who discuss the murder of Che even mention the American government's now widely-known practice from that period of political assassination (a practice that continues to this day). The United States participated in the murders or attempted murders of Kim Koo, Korean opposition leader (1949); Zhou Enlai, Prime Minister of China, (1950s); Sukarno, President of Indonesia (1950s); Kim Il Sung, Premier of North Korea (1951); Claro M. Recto, Philippines opposition leader (mid-1950s); Jawaharlal Nehru, Prime Minister of India (1955); Gamal Abdul Nasser, President of Egypt (1957); Norodom Sihanouk, leader of Cambodia (1959 and 1963); Brig. Gen. Abdul Karim Kassem, leader of Iraq (1960); Jose Figeres, President of Costa Rica, two attempts on his life (1950s-70s); Francois "Papa Doc" Duvalier, leader of Haiti (1961); Patrice Lumumba, Prime Minister of Congo (Zaire), (1961); Gen. Rafael Trujillo, leader of the Dominican Republic (1961); Ngo Dinh Diem, President of South Vietnam (1963); as listed in *Killing Hope*, William Blum, Common Courage Press, 1995.[19]

Moreover, none of these writers consider the CIA's own admission that it had tried to assassinate Che, as well as Fidel Castro and his brother Raul, on various occasions when they were in Cuba, as revealed in testimony from the Church Committee hearings[20]. This had been documented earlier in a secret 1967 CIA Inspector General's Report commissioned by then-CIA Director Richard Helms. It is published in its entirety and entitled "CIA Targets Fidel" (Ocean Press, 1994). As early as 1960, it was understood that it was necessary to assassinate Fidel, Raul, and Che if the Cuban Revolution was to be overthrown, and that without these three, the Cuban government would be leaderless. In a meeting on March 9, 1960, J. C. King, Chief of the CIA's Western Hemisphere Division, told the Task Force which was in charge of Cuban operations: "Unless Fidel and Raul Castro and Che Guevara could he eliminated in one package—which is highly unlikely—the operation can be a long, drawn-out affair and the present government will only be overthrown by the use of force." (Church Committee, Alleged Assassination Plots, p. 93).

The CIA report discusses the CIA's recruitment of the Chicago Mafia figure John Rosselli to do the job by poisoning Che and the Castros. The details of the plot arc instructive: "Harvey, the Support Chief (CIA) and Rosselli met for a second time in New York on April 8-9, 1962. (I.G. Report, p. 43) A notation made during this time in the files of the Technical Services Division indicates that four poison pills were given to the Support Chief on April 18, 1962. (I.G. Report, pp. 46–47) The pills were passed to Harvey who arrived in Miami on April 21, and found Rosselli already in touch with the same Cuban who had been involved in the pre-Bay of Pigs pill passage. (I.G. Report, p. 47) He gave the pills to Rosselli, explaining that "these would work anywhere and at any time with anything." (Rosselli, 6/24/75, p. 31) Rosselli testified that he told Harvey that the Cubans intended to use the pills to assassinate Che Guevara as well as Fidel and Raul Castro. According to Rosselli's testimony, Harvey approved of the targets, stating "everything is all right, what they want to do." (Rosselli, 6/24/75, p. 34) (Church Committee, Alleged Assassination Plots, p. 84)

The Church Committee also inquired as to what extent various Presidents including Eisenhower, Kennedy, and Johnson approved or were aware of these assassination plots. While it reaches no firm conclusion as to particular plots, a key CIA official testified that "generally that pursuant to the doctrine of 'plausible denial,' efforts are made that to keep matters that might be "embarrassing" away from Presidents".

Che's Death as Critical to U.S. "National Security Interests"

Most of these writers do not put Che's murder in the context of American policy in Cuba, Bolivia, or in Latin America at the time of his killing. It is a remarkable omission, which makes their conclusions suspect. Che's death was of crucial importance to United States' interests, as perceived by President Johnson, the national security establishment, the military, and the CIA. As U.S. government officials admitted at the time, "Che Guevara's death was a crippling—perhaps fatal—blow to the Bolivian guerilla movement and may prove a serious setback for Fidel Castro's hopes to foment violent revolution in all or almost all Latin American countries." [Document 33, pp. 148-151]

The U.S. role in Che's murder must be seen in the context of the 1959 Cuban revolution and the fears it engendered in the United States and among repressive governments in Latin America. The U.S. wanted to reverse what had happened in Cuba and, in this way, make it much less likely that other revolutions would succeed elsewhere.

One of the United States' responses to the Cuban revolution was the creation of the Alliance for Progress, a short-lived inter-American program initiated in 1961 after Cuba had been expelled from the Organization of American States. The program failed in its goal to relieve Latin American economic and social problems through loans which were supposed to increase per-capita income by 2.5% annually. Within ten years the U.S. began reducing the loans, relying instead on overt military repression. The escalating violence included covert CIA activity, attempted assassinations, and the training of Latin American police and military for counterinsurgency. The murder of Che, who was the embodiment of revolutionary change, was a critical part of this. Although there is no doubt the U.S. government did not want him to remain alive, they did not want to be implicated directly in aiding the Bolivians in the extermination of the guerillas or in Che's murder, for obvious reasons. Open U.S. intervention in Latin American affairs was regarded as unwise, for it would be seen as interference in the internal affairs of supposedly sovereign countries. Governments in Latin America risked anger from their populations if they openly appeared to do the bidding of the United States. Moreover, Che's killing was a cold-blooded murder, and as such, a war crime.

The U.S.'s success in defeating Che in Bolivia in 1967 was the high point of the counter-insurgency capability it had developed after the Cuban revolution to insure that no such revolutions would again occur. Che and Castro hoped that the Andes would become the Sierra Maestra of all of Latin America, a training ground for guerillas who would then spread the revolution from Bolivia to Chile, Argentina, Brazil, Ecuador, Peru, Venezuela, and throughout the entire subcontinent.

In Bolivia, Che sought to defend the gains of the Cuban revolution by extending it. He hoped to create "two, three, many Vietnams," in solidarity with the struggle in Indochina and as a means of weakening imperialism. Che wrote of the Cuban experience: "The example of our revolution and the lessons it applies for Latin America have destroyed all coffee house theories; we have demonstrated that a small group of men supported by the people and without fear of dying can overcome a disciplined regular army and defeat it."

For the United States the prospect that the spine of the Andes might turn out to be another Sierra Maestra of Latin America, with popular revolts leading to an armed socialist democracy, was indeed terrifying. Such a development would be a setback globally for the U.S., taking pressure off Vietnam, Cuba, El Salvador, Guatemala, Nicaragua and, above all, the Union of Soviet Socialist Republics. Thus, for Washington, defeating Che was crucial.

The Counterinsurgency Strategy

The strategy of counter-guerilla warfare that was successfully used against Che Guevara was first devised by the Kennedy/Johnson Administration when it took office in 1961. Walt Whitman Rostow was one of the architects of what became known as "Flexible Response." Rostow was one of President Lyndon Johnson's primary advisors, with an office in the White House. He had been recruited from the Massachusetts Institute of Technology by President Kennedy precisely to help devise a U.S. strategy to counter guerilla warfare. He coordinated a special group of military and intelligence officers that met weekly to monitor and to stop popular insurgencies worldwide. He specifically advised Johnson on Che's activity in Bolivia.

The incoming Kennedy administration began examining the tactics and strategy of the U.S. government in relation to the emergence of national liberation movements in the third world. They took note of the fact that China and then Cuba had been lost to the world market and that Vietnam and all of Southeast Asia might go the same way. From the end of the Second World War in 1945 to 1960, American had developed a military strategy based upon nuclear weaponry called "massive retaliation." It was centered on the possibility of a third world war, and in particular a showdown with the Soviet Union. It involved a build-up of a large armory of nuclear weapons, including intercontinental ballistic missiles and long-range bombers, all armed with nuclear warheads. If the Soviet Union were, in any way, to threaten the perimeters of the American Empire, it would suffer a devastating retaliatory strike.

Despite the Cuban Missile Crisis of 1962, when the Soviet Union's placement of missiles in Cuba in response to the Bay of Pigs invasion and the installing of U.S. missiles in Turkey prompted a nerve-wracking showdown between the superpowers, it was becoming increasingly apparent that direct conflict initiated by the Soviet Union was no longer a primary threat. As Che recognized, the Soviet Union had long since ceased its policy of revolutionary internationalism, preferring "peaceful" co-existence with the capitalist world and America in particular. Instead, the primary danger to U.S. interests came from forces seeking progressive change in the third world, and especially in Latin America, where revolutionary movements were emerging. A strategy had to be devised to cope with peasants who were armed only with primitive weaponry but who were not deterred by nuclear arsenals.

Chief of Staff General Maxwell Taylor, in his book *The Uncertain Trumpet*, presaged the entire shift in strategy. Taylor was one of the first to point out that the capacity for massive retaliation was of decreasing value and that what was required was 'flexible response.' "Massive retaliation as a driving strategic concept has reached a dead end," he wrote, calling instead for a "capability to cope with the entire spectrum of possible challenge." Taylor set off a chain of thinking that culminated in a report from a team headed by Henry Kissinger and financed by the Rockefeller Brothers' Fund. The report, "International Security: The Military Aspects," stated that mobile forces must be tailored to confront guerilla struggles, something that could not be done with nuclear weaponry.

This approach came to the fore under the Kennedy administration. Kennedy made Taylor his chief military advisor, brought in Robert McNamara from the Ford Motor Company as his Secretary of Defense, and Walt Rostow and McGeorge Bundy, from Harvard University, as advisors, all of whom supported the new strategy. But it was Kennedy himself who was the biggest proponent of the new approach. Speaking at West Point in 1962, he said: "subversive insurgency is another type of war, wholly new in its intensity, war by guerillas, by subversives, by insurgents, in short, by assassins, war by ambush instead of combat, by infiltration instead of aggression, seeking victory by erosion and exhausting the enemy, instead of honorably engaging him. It is in these situations where we need a wholly new kind of strategy, a wholly new kind of force, and therefore a new and wholly different kind of training."

As part of this approach Kennedy increased the Special Forces of the U.S. military fivefold. He wanted the force to be a dedicated, high-quality, elite corps of specialists, able to operate behind enemy lines, with sufficient expertise in guerilla warfare that they could train local forces, as the Green Berets were to do in Bolivia in 1967.

Kennedy looked at the current military manuals and saw that none of them contained any information about counterinsurgency. He began to read Mao and Che himself, and made sure that foreign and military officers who were stationed in third-world countries were given their writings on guerilla warfare. Using the pretext of a contrived crisis over access to Berlin in 1961, he was able to persuade Congress to increase the military budget by 3.6 billion dollars and increase the armed forces from 2,500,000 to 2,750,000. All kinds of new, non-nuclear weapons were added. This began a general military escalation that, by 1964, included an 800% increase in the Special Forces trained to deal with counterinsurgency threats.

In the summer of 1962, President Kennedy instituted the Special Group on Counter-Insurgency. Headed by Taylor and including Rostow, it met in the White House every week and continued to do so after Kennedy's death, through the Johnson years, up to and past the time of Che's murder. One particularly important part of the strategy it devised, that of "rapid deployment," was based on McNamara's understanding of the implications of Che's call for "two, three many Vietnams." This, should it ever come about, would pose a serious threat to the U.S. military by stretching its manpower and resources beyond the breaking point. Rapid deployment was designed to nip guerilla activity in the bud, so that major fighting on several fronts simultaneously could be avoided. McNamara testified before the U.S. Senate in 1965, the year before Che's entrance into Bolivia, that the "first few weeks of a limited war conflict are usually the most critical. Thus the ability to concentrate our military power in a matter of days rather than weeks can make an enormous difference in the total force ultimately required and in some cases serves to halt aggression before it really gets started." With respect to Che in Bolivia, this would prove prophetic.

Che's Early Background

Che's parents eloped when his mother was three-months pregnant. His parents were off-beat Argentine aristocrats with more blue blood than money. One ancestor had been the Spanish Royal Viceroy of Colonial Peru and another had been an Argentine general. His mother's father was a renowned law professor, congressman, and ambassador. Che, born in 1928, was the oldest of five children. He contracted lifelong, debilitating asthma at age two, causing the family to move from Buenos Aires to the healthier high altitudes of the provinces. Because of his asthma, much of Che's education was at home. Later, his poor health also resulted in him being rejected by the draft. The great warrior of the Cuban revolution was found to have "diminished physical abilities," and Che told his friends that he "thanked his shitty lungs for doing something useful for a change.[21]"

Che's mother Celia ran a bohemian household. Books and magazines covered the furniture. People stopped by to discuss and smoke and drink red wine. There were no discernible fixed mealtimes. The children rode their bikes through the living room into the backyard. Che's parents were anti-clerical in a conservative neighborhood. The children played soccer after school, with teams made up of those who believed in God and those who did not. Those who did not usually lost because their team was invariably smaller. Che's parents were also political, and, along with Che, actively opposed the Franco dictatorship in fascist Spain. While in college, Che denounced Nazi professors at the university. When in his teens, Che wrote poetry and five philosophical notebooks. He read assiduously and kept an index of the literature he had read by author, nationality, title and genre. He read the entire 25-volume contemporary history of the modern world owned by his father, as well as the collected works of Jules Verne, Sigmund Freud, Bertrand Russell, Aldous Huxley, Benito Mussolini, Joseph Stalin, Emile Zola, Jack London, and Vladimir Ilyich Lenin. He read the *Communist Manifesto*, dipped into *Das Kapital*, and in his third philosophical journal wrote a long piece on Marx's life and works. He intended to write a biography of Marx. He also wrote a portrait of Lenin, whom he appreciated as a person who "lived, breathed, and slept" socialist revolution[22].

Che got a summer job shipping out with the merchant marine, where he rubbed shoulders with all sorts of people. Traveling and keeping a journal became a lifelong habit. His *Motorcycle Diaries,* published in 1993, were widely read and then made into a popular movie of the same name. The book describes how, in 1952, Che headed across Argentina and towards Chile with his friend, Alberto Granado, on an old Norton 500cc motorcycle, free-loading food and lodging whenever they could. Che's dad had given him a pistol to use against danger. One night, they had been courteously extended the use of a farmer's barn. Che lay awake looking out into the darkness when suddenly he saw the fiery eyes of a puma, a South American mountain lion. He squeezed off a shot and killed the beast. In the morning when he awoke he discovered that he had, in fact, killed the farmer's dog[23]. Che visited the copper mines in Chile and tin mines in Bolivia. With his characteristically caustic tongue, he commented that the Yankees had taken everything and left to the native people "only an ox."

Upon his return from his motorcycle odyssey, Che demonstrated his extraordinary capacity for learning by passing ten different medical school exams in as many weeks, and becoming a doctor: "I dreamed of becoming a famous investigator... of working indefatigably to find something that could be definitively placed at the disposition of humanity." In fact, it was as a revolutionary, rather than as a doctor, that the world came to know Che.

Guatemala

In 1953, at the age of 25, Che left Argentina for good, ending up in the small Central America state of Guatemala. Seven months after he arrived there, the CIA succeeded in overthrowing the elected government of Jacobo Arbenz. A reformer, Arbenz had stepped on corporate America's toes by nationalizing some of the vast unused land holdings of the United Fruit Company. The United States recruited Castillo Armas, an ex-Army colonel and a furniture salesman, and supplied him with arms and training in neighboring Nicaragua, then under the rule of the dictator Somoza. Armas' troops took over Guatemala with little resistance, and the 25-year-old Argentine physician was forced to flee to Mexico with his new wife, the Peruvian Marxist Hilda Gadea, getting out of the country just in the nick of time. Hilda was more experienced politically than Che. She helped educate him and bore him a daughter, Hildita, who was born soon after their escape.

Fidel, in his spoken autobiography, writes that some of those Cubans who attacked the Moncada barracks in Cuba on July 26, 1953, had escaped to Guatemala and met Che when he was there during the Arbenz period. (*Fidel Castro, My Life* by Fidel Castro & Ignacio Ramonet, p. 172) After Arbenz's overthrow they went together to Mexico where in July of 1955 Che met Fidel in Mexico City. Although we have no document from a U.S. agency regarding his stay in Guatemala contemporaneous to that time, documents from 1956 discuss his presence in Guatemala. **[Documents 2 and 3, pp. 89-90]** The earliest document concerning Che is his "Bio Data" sheet and a copy of his passport from his 1952 entry into the U.S. **[Document 1 p. 88]**

Mexico

After meeting Fidel in Mexico City, Che described him as "...a young man, intelligent, very sure of himself and of extraordinary audacity: I think there is a mutual sympathy between us.[24]" They went out for dinner, and after talking for hours, Fidel invited Che to join his guerilla movement. Che accepted on the spot. He was the second person to do so. The first was Raul Castro, Fidel's younger brother. Che wrote, "The truth is that after the experiences of my wanderings across all of Latin America, and to top it off, in Guatemala, it didn't take much to incite me to join any revolution against a tyrant, but Fidel impressed me as an extraordinary man. He faced and overcame the most impossible things. He had an exceptional faith in that once he left for Cuba he would arrive. And that once he arrived, he would fight. And that fighting, he would win. I shared his optimism... [it was time to] stop crying and fight."

The profound historical understandings about the poor countries of the Americas and the Caribbean, which Fidel shared with Che in Mexico City were: (1) The monopoly land-holdings had to be broken up and given to the peasants who work them, (2) the population had to be armed to defend their conquest, and (3) the old ruling repressive apparatus had to be eliminated.

According to Fidel, Che, in their first meeting together, asked him to make only one promise: "The only thing I ask is that when the Revolution triumphs in Cuba, you not forbid me for reasons of state, from going to Argentina to make a revolution there. (Fidel Castro, *My Life* p. 174) Fidel agreed especially as he and others were at that time "carrying out an incipient but strong policy of internationalism." (Fidel Castro, *My Life* p. 174) Fidel also talks in this book about Che's military training in Mexico. Che and the others were trained by a Spanish General who had been born in Cuba in 1892. Interestingly, that general,

Alberto Bayo, had fought in the Spanish Civil War against Franco and fled to Mexico after the defeat of the Republicans.

On June 20, 1956, Fidel and two comrades were arrested on a street in downtown Mexico City. Four days later, on June 24, Che too was taken into custody. Che's arrest is noted in a U.S. document, which says he was "arrested in Mexico in connection with the Fidel Castro plot against President Batista of Cuba." [**Document 2, p. 89**] There is a similar document of roughly the same date regarding Che's spouse Hilda Gadea de Guevara, although she was not arrested. [**Document 3, p. 90**] Within days, all the members of the newly formed 'July 26th movement' were "accused of plotting Batista's assassination in collusion Cuban and Mexican Communists . . . Havana had demanded their extradition." (Anderson, 189) Che was placed in the jail of the Interior Ministry. He told them he was a tourist, that he had come from Guatemala and admitted liking Arbenz. He was charged with violating Mexico's immigration laws, although the press sensationalized the story, labeling Che and some twenty other arrested comrades as Communist plotters. Finally, after some two months in jail, Che was released—possibly, as Anderson reports, because Fidel had paid a bribe.

The Sierra Maestra

On November 25, 1956, Che, acting as the troop's doctor, left from Mexico for Cuba with Fidel and 82 guerillas on the motor launch, *Granma*. Batista was forewarned of the invasion, both because of an ill-timed urban uprising in Cuba as well as the spotting of the *Granma* by a Cuban ship. The Granma landed at an unplanned spot in a mango swamp. Batista's soldiers were there to meet it. Only 22 of the men on board survived the ambush and they scattered into the Sierra Maestra mountains. Che was caught up in the ambush but escaped. Faced with a split-second decision, he grabbed a box of ammunition rather than his medical kit[25]. His skills as a warrior were recognized by others, and Fidel promoted him to commandante. As the war developed, Che became Fidel's chief confidant as well as his de facto military chief of staff. He began a relationship with a woman who fought alongside of him, Aleida March. After Che divorced Hilda, they married and subsequently had two sons and two daughters.

During the revolutionary war, Che's father, brimming with admiration, told of a reporter who wrote how busy Che was: "[He] had laid the bases for agrarian reform in the Sierra; built an arms factory; invented a bazooka rifle; inaugurated the first bread factory in the mountains; built and equipped a hospital; created the first school and installed a radio transmitter called Radio Rebelde... and he still had time left to found a small newspaper to inform the rebel troops.[26]"

In 1958 the CIA sent a spy—posing as a journalist—into Che's camp in the Sierra Maestra where he headed Column IV (so-called though there were only two columns) a year before the revolution. The subsequent CIA report states that Che was "anti-American." [**Document 9, p. 105**] The spy actually slept for a week in Che's tent. He smells, the spy reported, and he smokes long cigars in the evening and regularly reads to his troops. That week he was reading Daudet. "He is pretty intellectual for a Latino," the agent wrote. [**Document 6e, p. 99**] Another CIA report describes Che as believing himself to be acting in the "tradition of Simon Bolivar." [**Document 4, pp. 91-92**] A later CIA report states that Guevara says he defended Arbenz so Guatemala could defend itself against "exploitation by foreign capital." [**Document 10, pp. 106-108**]

Together with Camilo Cienfuegos, Che led the troops at the famous battle of Santa Clara, an operation that cut the island in half, insuring the rebel victory. The revolutionaries marched into Havana on Jan. 8, 1959. Che was a hero of the war. A law had to be passed lowering the minimum age of holding office from 35 to 30 so that Fidel could assume the post of prime minister. He was 32 at the time. Che was 30. Another law was passed making Che a citizen of Cuba.

The success of the Fidelista overthrow of the American-supported Batista dictatorship seems miraculous. The tiny guerilla force succeeded against 50,000 U.S.-trained and -supplied troops, but the government had few allies among the people. The guerillas had massive support throughout the cities and countryside, and in the end there was little Batista could do except quietly board a flight and escape to Miami.

After the Revolution

After the revolution triumphed, the CIA continued to track Che, making note of his positions and activities. [**Documents 11-16, pp. 109-117**] Che became the head of the La Cabana Fortress, where the Batista counter-revolutionaries and torturers were imprisoned. Appointing Miguel Angel Duque de Estrada as head of the Comision de Depuracion ("Cleansing Commission"), Che took overall responsibility for organizing the trials of these men and was scrupulous in attempting to ensure the judgments passed were objective. Over the course of three months several hundred prisoners across Cuba were found guilty of murder or torture and were executed, some 55 at La Cabana[27].

Che prepared Cuba's agrarian reform law and designed the agency that would implement it. The law was very popular because a lot of Cubans who had fought on the side of the revolution benefited directly from it. Previously, large tracts of land had been owned by American corporations. The average Cuban peasant worked part-time, seasonally, was not literate, and lived from hand to mouth. The revolutionary government nationalized these big properties—something it was entitled to do under international law. The former owners were told they would be compensated for their losses. The American owners were advised that they would be paid exactly the amount they declared their properties were worth when they listed them for tax purposes. The offers of the Cuban government were turned down by these owners.

In retaliation, the United States, which hitherto had processed all of Cuba's oil in American-owned refineries, stopped doing so, and Cuba was cut off from gasoline. The Cubans, in turn, responded by nationalizing the refineries, the bus company, the phone company, the nickel mines, and the economy in general. Instead of production for profit, a planned economy was created. This was the Cuban socialist revolution. The response of the United States was to begin a blockade, in October 1960.

The following April, Cuban mercenaries organized by the United States invaded Cuba at Playa Giron (The Bay of Pigs). They were defeated within 72 hours. The economic blockade was fully in place by February 1962 and has continued to the present[28].

The blockade has had devastating consequences on the island. It has been accompanied by continuing acts of violence against the Cuban people, as evidenced by a 1999 lawsuit brought against the U.S. government. The lawsuit, for $181 billion in damages, was filed in Havana by eight organizations in Cuba, including trade unions, groups of small farmers, the women's organization, the children's organization, the Committees to Defend the Revolution, and the veterans. These organizations make up most of the Cuban population. The suit alleged and identified acts of aggression by the U.S., its agents, servants, and employees, from the period of 1960 to 1999. Among a litany of charges the document averred that the U.S. was responsible over these four decades for killing 3,498 persons in Cuba and injuring 2,099 more. The suit charged that the U.S. launched and supported air and naval attacks against Cuba, machine gun attacks on people in Havana and on passenger trains, supported armed terrorist groups in the countryside, the Bay of Pigs invasion, the bombing of a Cubana airliner in 1976 in which 73 people were killed, and the infliction of emotional suffering from acts of terrorism. It asserted that the U.S. launched biological warfare causing dengue fever, often fatal to children, and the introduction of swine flu which killed 500,000 pigs. The suit alleged that the U.S. supported terrorists who murdered teachers and attacked collective farms, setting fire to the sugar crops and killing people in the process. This lawsuit and its outcome is described in *Washington on Trial: The People of Cuba vs. the U.S. Government*, edited by David Deutschmann and Michael Ratner (Ocean Press, 1999).

In the six years Che spent in Cuba before he left in 1965—first to fight in the Congo, and then Bolivia—he headed up Cuba's National Bank; traveled extensively; successfully concluded trade deals around the world; served as a spokesperson for Cuba, with notable élan at the United Nations; and headed Cuba's industrialization effort in order to get away from a dependent one-crop export economy. He wrote the classic manual *On Guerilla Warfare*, which was read intently on both sides of the class line, by revolutionaries as well as the American military.

Che spoke widely throughout Cuba, speeches which were either monitored by or recorded by informants working with the CIA and the FBI. While accepting an honorary degree at the University of Las Villas in December of 1959, Che told the gathered faculty and students that the days when education was a privilege of the white middle classes had ended. "The University," he said, "must paint itself black, mulatto, worker and peasant." If it didn't, he warned, "the people would break down its doors . . . and paint the University the colors they liked.[29]" In a speech at Havana University in 1962, he spoke of the role of students in the revolutionary process. Che emphasized that there are "those who, although coming from a social class which has been destroyed, are capable of understanding the historical necessity and absolute impossibility of changing what has occurred in Cuba—students who want to join the revolution." (*Che Guevara and the FBI*, p. 85)

Che In Africa I: The Algiers Speech February, 1965

In the early part of 1965, Che travelled to Africa to engage with the liberation struggles that were taking place in a number of countries there. He visited an MPLA camp located in the Congo-Brazzaville Republic, a trip closely followed by U.S. spy agencies. [**Document 17, pp. 118-119**] The MPLA was the guerilla group fighting for the liberation of Angola from Portugal. Che's speech to the MPLA stated that Cuba is "entirely with you, the Angolan people, with the people of Mozambique and of the so called Portuguese Guinea." Che then emphasized that the most difficult problem in winning a guerilla war "is that the man in the mountains must be made into a guerilla." A guerilla is one "who has learned not to fear the army of the enemy." "We were not an army of heroes. Far from it. But at the end, a relatively small group completely defeated the army of tyranny."

Che's last public speech, widely recognized as one of his most important, was given in Algiers in February 1965, at the Second Economic Seminar on Afro-Asian Solidarity. Che spoke movingly of the need for international solidarity in the struggle against imperialism: "[B]ecause there are no frontiers in the struggle to the death, we cannot remain indifferent in the face of what occurs in any part of the world. A victory for any country against imperialism is our victory, just as any country's defeat is a defeat for us all. The practice of internationalism is not only a duty for the peoples who struggle for a better future; it is also an inescapable necessity." (*Che Guevara Reader*, Ocean Press, 1997)

While Che acknowledged Soviet military aid and a generous Soviet trade agreement that subsidized Cuba's sugar exports, his speech in Algiers criticized the Soviet Union for insufficiently supporting the Vietnamese and taking competitive advantage of Third World countries—in short, as he said, for being "an accomplice with imperialism." It was at this conference that Che said the socialist countries "have the moral duty to liquidate their tacit complicity with Western countries." The speech was a slap in the face for those in Moscow who favored peaceful coexistence." Che advocated extending the revolution to protect Cuba's gains and to offer solidarity with the embattled Vietnamese.

Che arrived back in Cuba on March 14, 1965, and disappeared from public sight towards the end of March. He never again publicly appeared in Cuba.

Rumors of a Split with Fidel

Some commentators have claimed that the Algiers speech angered Fidel, as Cuba was relying upon aid from some of the socialist countries Che criticized, and that the speech was therefore a factor in Che's leaving Cuba. However, these commentators have taken parts of the speech out of context. Che also said that the Soviet Union and China were "the most generous toward the third world." Other evidence demonstrates that Che was preparing to leave Cuba long before this speech and for reasons unrelated to any supposed disagreements with Fidel.

Che clearly left Cuba to fight in and lead liberation struggles. In almost every speech he gave, he exhorted people to fight against imperialism and to do so with armed struggle. He saw the fight as a worldwide necessity, and Cuba as an example to be emulated. It is known that he was planning a Bolivian and Latin American guerilla strategy since at least as early as 1962 and probably before. Tania (Tamara Bunke), the revolutionary who was with him in Bolivia, was trained in Cuba. She had met Che in 1964 in East Germany and in that meeting Che explained that her mission was to go to Bolivia.

The CIA files reflect the vast rumor-mongering that spread worldwide as to whether Che and Fidel had split, or worse. An October 1965 Intelligence Memorandum entitled the "The Fall of Che Guevara" asserts that Fidel had dropped Guevara who had fallen from power because of his opposition to "the practical policies recommended by the Soviet Union." Other information collected by the spy agencies asserted that Che had been assassinated by the Soviets and that he had a violent political argument with Fidel and was probably killed as a result[30].

The truth is that there was no split. When Che joined up with Fidel and the Cubans in Mexico City in 1956, it was with the understanding that if they succeeded in Cuba, Che was free to move on. The Cubans embraced Che's internationalism, as evidenced by their efforts in Algeria, the Congo and Bolivia.

Fidel not only supported Che's Bolivian campaign but followed it on an almost daily basis as long as there was radio contact. In the final days of the Bolivian campaign when there had been no news about Che, Fidel visited regularly with Che's family worrying about the outcome. In addition, despite Soviet objections to Che's presence in Bolivia and the possibility of serious harm to Cuba's economic ties to the Soviet Union, Fidel insisted on Cuba's support for Che and the Latin American revolutionary movements.

This support is summarized in **Document 36, pp. 156-157** a CIA Intelligence Information Cable, dated October 17, 1967, a few days after Che's murder. The document recounts the history of the discussions between Fidel and the Soviet Union on the subject of Cuba's attitude towards Che and revolutions in Bolivia and elsewhere. This document is of historic significance. An alarmed Soviet government, upon learning that Che was in Bolivia, sent Soviet Premier Aleksey Kosygin to visit Fidel in Havana from June 26th to June 30th of 1967. In all likelihood using electronic surveillance the CIA was able to listen in on the discussions, and sent condensed transcripts to the White House and the Army, among other places. Kosygin's purpose in speaking with Castro was to express his government's opposition to Che's presence in Bolivia and Castro's policy of supporting revolutionary activity in Latin America. He objected to the fact that his government was not told of the Bolivian initiative beforehand and that the guerilla effort was 'playing into the hands of the imperialists,' and was weakening and diverting the efforts of the 'Socialist World,' that is, those Latin American communist parties loyal to Moscow, in its efforts to 'liberate' Latin America.

Castro did not accept Kosygin's premise that the Communist Party of the Soviet Union and its followers in Latin America were revolutionary. This CIA document shows succinctly how conscious the American intelligence agency was of the differences between Cuba and the Soviet Union and where the U.S. interests lay. The CIA knew that Cuba did not agree with the Soviet approach to "Wars of National Liberation" in Latin America. It stated that Castro "[a]ccused the U.S.S.R. of having turned its back upon its own revolutionary tradition and of having moved to a point where it would refuse to support any revolutionary movement unless the actions of the latter contributed to the achievement of Soviet objectives, as contrasted to international Communist objectives." This document effectively puts to rest any questions regarding a split with Fidel or claims that Fidel did not support Che in Bolivia.

Che in Africa II, July 1965

After Che's Algiers speech, in which he expressed enthusiasm for the revolutionary possibilities in Africa, Fidel raised the idea that Che return to Africa to lead the Cuban guerilla contingent already in training for a mission to the Congo. Che left in April 1965. According to Miguel "Red Beard" Pinero, then head of Cuba's overseas revolutionary activities, "Che didn't need much convincing. [He] came back really enthused by his contacts with the Africans. So Fidel told him 'why don't you go to Africa?' He was really restless with the passing of time and his inability to fulfill what he saw as his historic mission.[31]"

The Congo Mission to defeat the Western-backed Tshombe regime did not succeed. The rebellion Che joined was led by the political heirs of Patrice Lumumba, the Congo's first Prime Minister, who had who had been murdered by Tshombe's forces, most likely with U.S. collusion, in 1961. By the time Che arrived, the rebellion was almost over and it was unlikely much could have been done, despite the Cuban support. In addition, the Congolese rebel leadership, including Laurent Kabila, remained disorganized and uncooperative[32]. During this period the world-wide rumor-mongering and wild speculation as to Che's whereabouts and his relations with Fidel and the Cuban Revolution were such that Fidel felt compelled to make public a farewell letter that Che had written to him before leaving for Africa. The CIA was aware that Fidel was seeking to quell the speculation about Che. This is reflected in an Intelligence Information Cable dated September 28, 1965, in which Fidel is reported to have announced that a document explaining Che's absence would be read at a public event. [**Document 16, p. 117**]

Fidel read out Che's letter at a rally on October 3, after introducing the Central Committee of the newly created Communist Party of Cuba. "Other regions of the world claim the support of my modest efforts. I can do what is forbidden to you because of your responsibility to Cuba, and the time has come for us to separate . . . On new battlefields I will carry with me the faith that you have inculcated in me, the revolutionary spirit of my people, the feeling of having fulfilled the most sacred of duties: to fight imperialism wherever it may be[33] . . ."

Che and the CIA in Bolivia

After the letter was made public and the possibilities in the Congo had been exhausted, Che did not want to return in any public capacity to Cuba. He had given up his honorary Cuban citizenship and all his official positions and had cast his lot with world revolution. When Che did return from Africa briefly for training in Cuba in 1966, his presence on the island was not made public. There is much speculation in the CIA documents at that time over his whereabouts, but they truly did not know where he was. Although Che was not yet in Bolivia, a CIA document of April 23, 1966, titled "Revolutionary Group Allegedly Bound for Bolivia" states that 90 "Cuban-trained revolutionaries" are going to Bolivia and that Che Guevara is leading a force of guerillas in the Andes. [**Document 18, p. 120**]. Che's preparations, including the setting up of a clandestine network in La Paz, had been in the works for some years, and the CIA evidently had some inkling of his plans.

Why did Che choose Bolivia? Landlocked, Bolivia was Latin America's poorest, most illiterate, most rural and most Indian country. It was also the most unstable country in Latin America, having gone through 189 changes in government since it became an independent republic in 1825. Like Mexico in the years 1910 to 1920, and Cuba more recently, Bolivia was a Latin American country whose revolution in 1952 was based on popular participation. And, of course, Bolivia is a neighbor to Che's home country of Argentina.

Constantio Apasa, a Bolivian tin miner, summed up the political situation in his country in the year that Che arrived: "When the MNR (Revolutionary Nationalist Movement) came to power in 1952, we felt it was a workers' party and things would be different. But then the MNR politicians organized a secret police and filled their pockets. They rebuilt the army which we had destroyed, and when it got big enough, the army threw them out. Now the army has new weapons which we cannot match.[34]" The 1964 military coup ended the MNR's twelve year reign. The military officers who now ran Bolivia were all U.S.-trained.

Che arrived in Bolivia via Uruguay in early November of 1966 disguised as a Uruguayan businessman. So deceptive was his appearance—shaved beard, horn-rimmed glasses, tailored bank suit—that Phil Agee, the CIA agent in Uruguay charged with finding Che, (who was to quit the agency soon thereafter and become a supporter of the Cuban Revolution), wrote that Che easily avoided Uruguayan officials despite a warning leaflet Agee had prepared and passed out at the airport in Montevideo. In fact, Fidel told author Ignacio Ramonet that even Raul Castro failed to recognize Che upon meeting him before he left Cuba for Bolivia[35].

Che's plan was to set up a camp for his guerillas and, once they were trained, move his troops north to engage the weak Bolivian army. On November 7, 1966, Che arrived at the guerilla base on the Nacahuazu River in Bolivia. It is the first date in Che's *Bolivian Diary*, and opens with: "Today begins a new phase. We arrived at the farm at night. The trip went quite well." (*The Bolivian Diary*, p. 35 Ocean Press, 2006). They were to train for approximately four months before engaging in battle. We have no U.S. government documents from roughly the day Che arrived in Bolivia until some four months later. It seems probable that the U.S. did not know his whereabouts during this time. We have used Che's diary to fill in this gap.

What follows are shortened versions of Che's monthly summaries for November, December, January, and February, 1967. During this period the guerillas were training, scouting terrain, and preparing themselves for battle. Che was holding secret meetings with Mario Monje, head of the Communist Party of Bolivia, who ultimately refused to support the expedition. Che noted in his diary that "the party is now taking up ideological arms against us."

At the end of November Che writes: "Everything has gone quite well; my arrival was without incident. . . . The general outlook seems good in this remote region[36]. . . ." By the end of December "the team of Cubans has been successfully completed; morale is good and there are only minor problems. The Bolivians are doing well, although only few in number.[37]" At the end of January:

"Now the real guerilla phase begins and we will test the troops; time will tell what they can do and what the prospects for the Bolivian revolution are. Of everything that was envisioned, the slowest has been the incorporation of Bolivian combatants.[38]" On February 1, Che took most of the men on what was supposed to be a two-week training mission. It turned into an almost 50-day ordeal in which two of the Bolivians drowned. At the end of February, while still on the training mission, Che wrote: "Although I have no news of what is happening at the camp, everything is going reasonably well, with some exceptions, fatal in one instance. . . . The next phase will be combat, and will be decisive.[39]"

By the middle of the following month things had stopped "going reasonably well." On March 16, three days before Che and his guerillas returned to the camp, two men, Vincente Rocabado Terrazas and Pastor Barrera Quintana, deserted from the party that had been left behind. They were picked up and interrogated by the Bolivian authorities. They gave information about the guerillas and their location. As a result, the police raided a farm where some of the guerillas were stationed. From then on, Che and his guerillas were effectively on the run. The Bolivian army was scouring the area, and those who had stayed behind saw a plane circling above the area over a period of days.

The report from the deserters caused alarm at the highest levels of the Bolivian government, as is set forth in a Department of State telegram to the Secretary of State and others from the U.S. Ambassador to Bolivia, Douglas Henderson. Henderson had been ambassador to Bolivia since 1963, a year before the Bolivian revolution was overthrown in 1964. He was a career foreign-service officer whose father had joined the U.S. Army and helped put down the Philippine insurrection of 1899-1902, as well as the Mexican Revolution in 1916. Henderson's telegram describes a meeting held on March 17. [**Document 19, pp. 121-122**] The meeting was between President Barrientos, his acting chief of the armed forces and other Bolivian military officials on the one side, and on the other side, Henderson, his Deputy Chief of Mission and the Defense Attaché.

The subject of the memo is "Reported Guerilla Activity in Bolivia." It opens with a reference to a phone call to the ambassador. "At the urgent request of President Barrientos, I called on him at his house this afternoon." In substance, Henderson's telegram reports the capture of the two deserters, their admitted association with about 40 guerillas, and their location. The deserters said they were led by Castroite Cubans and the contingent included other nationalities. The two men mentioned Che Guevara as the leader but admitted they had never seen him. Both Henderson and Barrientos were doubtful of Guevara's presence. Barrientos "requested immediate assistance, especially radio locating equipment to help pin-point reported guerilla radio transmitters." Henderson responds by making no commitments and says to Washington that "we are taking this report of guerilla activity with some reserve." But he says he will try and furnish the radio equipment locally before asking for further help.

Barrientos had come to power in the typical Bolivian manner: The democratically-elected government of Victor Paz Estenssoro was overthrown in November of 1964 by a U.S.-supported coup, which Barrientos led. The CIA and the Pentagon wanted Paz out. In 1964, Paz had voted to keep Cuba in the Organization of American States and against the U.S.-sponsored OAS sanctioning of Cuba, refusing to break relations between his country and the beleaguered island. Che called the OAS the "Ministry of Colonies." Barrientos had trained in the United States and had a close relationship with both the CIA and the American military. His friend and flight instructor while he trained in America was Colonel Edward Fox, who was the military attaché at the American embassy in La Paz in 1964. At that time Fox worked for the CIA.

Twenty of the twenty-three top Bolivian military men now running the country were trained by the United States at the School of the Americas then in the Panama Canal Zone, as were 1,200 officers and men in the Bolivian armed forces. The School of the Americas trained and indoctrinated so many Latin American military men it was known throughout Latin America as the "Escuela de Golpes" (Coup School). Recent events in Vietnam were very much on Ambassador Henderson's mind, and he was wary of Barrientos. He stood for a more measured response to the guerillas than the hard-line approach suggested by the Bolivian president. He believed that "overkill" could easily make the Bolivian peasantry into durable enemies of the United States.

In a survey of instability across Latin America in 1965, the CIA ranked Bolivia second only to the Dominican Republic, which they were to invade that year. The Agency was afraid that the political turmoil in Bolivia could lead to communists toppling Barrientos. Through Henderson, Barrientos requested that the United States provide the Bolivian army with high-performance aircraft and napalm as well as the radio locators. He also asked Henderson to warn the governments of Paraguay and Argentina about the guerilla threat, which he did. However, on Henderson's advice, the U.S put off supplying aircraft and napalm, fearing that their use would likely prove counterproductive by turning the peasantry toward Che.

On March 19, Che arrived back at the guerilla's base camp after the lengthy training mission that had gone awry. Upon his return he received the bad news about the two desertions. Che, too, had seen a plane circling the day before and was concerned. He was told the news that the police had raided the farm and that the army could be advancing against them.

He met with Tania Benke, the undercover operative who had been sent to La Paz two years earlier as support for Che, who had arrived at the camp during his absence. Tania was thirty-two years old and had grown up in Argentina, where her parents were refugees from Nazi Germany. Her father, a language teacher, was German; her mother was a Russian Jew. Both were Communists. Tania first met Che in 1959 when he led a delegation to East Germany and she was a philosophy student at Humboldt University in East Berlin. She moved to Cuba two years later where she attended the University of Havana, worked in the Ministry of Education, and joined the Cuban Women's Militia before leaving for Bolivia.

Tania had arrived at the camp in February along with Regis Debray and Ciro Bustos. Debray was to have been Che's courier to Havana and then to Paris. He came from an upper-class Parisian family and had attended the prestigious Ecole normale superieure. Debray had recently taught philosophy in Havana and had written the widely-read book *Revolution in the Revolution*, which laid out what became the Fidelista theory of revolution—small groups of guerillas operating in the countryside and linking with supporters in the cities in a way that provided a catalyst for the seizure of power. The Leninist concept of building a mass socialist party was discarded. Debray popularized Guevara's argument that such a party was not necessary at this late stage of imperialism. In situations such as Bolivia where the government and its army were extremely weak and the American military stretched thin with 500,000 troops bogged down in Vietnam, a rural guerilla force with support in the urban areas could come to power without building a party of the Leninist type. This is what, Guevara argued, had happened in Cuba.

Tania had arranged false documents for Debray and Bustos, an Argentinian artist and an early supporter of the Cuban revolution who had travelled to Cuba in 1960, met Che, and collaborated with him in organizing support for revolutionaries in Uruguay before going to Bolivia. Despite Che's orders to the contrary, Tania had herself accompanied the men from La Paz to the Camiri guerilla camp. While she waited for Che, her jeep was discovered by the Bolivian army. It tied her to both the guerillas and the support network in La Paz. Che wrote: "Everything indicates that Tania has become known, which means that two years of good patient work has been lost. Departure has become very difficult now.[40]"

A few days after Che's return to the base camp, early on the morning of March 23, 1967, the guerillas fought their first battle. Che had sent out some of his men to set up a defensive perimeter. In the course of doing so they sprung an ambush on a group of Bolivian soldiers, killing seven and capturing eighteen. As Che reports, "Two prisoners—a major and a captain—talked like parrots.[41]" After this battle, it was obvious to Che that his general whereabouts had been discovered. This meant he and his men had to stay on the move.

A U.S. Department of Defense Intelligence Information Report dated March 31, 1967, on the subject of counterinsurgency capabilities in Bolivia reports in detail on this March 23 battle. [**Document 21, pp. 125-126**] "After diminishing reports of guerilla activity during the weekend of 17-21 March 1967, on March 23 a Bolivian army patrol clashed with a guerilla group ranging in reported numbers from 50-400. This action occurred in Nancahausu (1930S/6340W). . . .They are a well organized force and are armed with modern weapons and under the direction of Castroite Cubans. . . . The Bolivian Army has approximately 600 men involved at the present time . . . They are being supported by the Air Force. . . ."

The success of Che's forces caused alarm to Bolivian officials. On the day of the battle, Barrientos had another meeting with the U.S. Deputy Chief of Mission advising him that the guerilla situation had worsened, and that he believed the guerillas were "part of a large subversive movement led by Cuban and other foreigners." Barrientos said his troops were "green and ill-equipped" and asked again for urgent U.S. assistance. The recent attacks led the U.S. officials to believe that the guerillas "could constitute potential security threat to the Government of Bolivia."[**Documents 20, 21, pp. 123-126**] This Intelligence Information Report also points out "That the United States is the only foreign country providing military assistance and hardware to Bolivia." [**Document 21**]

Henderson and Barrientos met again on March 27, 1967. In a one and one-half hour meeting Barrientos appealed for direct U.S. aid to support the Bolivian armed forces so they could meet the "emergency" in which Bolivia was "helping to fight for the U.S." [**Document 20, pp. 123-124**] The Department of State responded to Henderson by saying it was reluctant to support a significantly enlarged army, but would provide a "limited amount of essential material to assist a carefully orchestrated response to the threat." If that proved inadequate, Henderson was to assure Barrientos that the U.S. would consider further requests for help. [**Document 20**] On March 31, 1967, the Department of State informed U.S. embassies in neighboring countries that the plan was to "block the guerilla escape, then bring in, train and prepare a ranger-type unit to eliminate the guerillas." Further, the Department of State was considering using a special U.S. Military Training Team "for accelerated training [of the] counter- guerilla force." [**Document 20**]

In reporting on this meeting, Henderson noted the sad state of the Bolivian armed forces: "I suspect that Barrientos is beginning to suffer some genuine anguish over the sad spectacle offered by the poor performance of his armed forces in this episode; i.e., an impetuous foray into reported guerilla country, apparently based on a fragment of intelligence and resulting in a minor disaster, which further tended to panic the GOB into a lather of ill-coordinated activity, with less than adequate professional planning and logistical support." [**Document 20**]

Che's analysis in his diary entry at the end of March included, among other points, an assessment of the overall situation: "General panorama is characterized as follows: The phase of consolidation and purging of the guerilla force—fully completed. The initial phase of the struggle, characterized by a precise and spectacular blow [the battle of March 23. 1967], but marked by gross indecision before and after the fact. . . . [bad conduct and missed opportunities by two of the guerillas]." He concluded that "evidently, we will have to hit the road before I expected and move on, leaving a group to recover, saddled with the burden of four possible informers. The situation is not good, but now begins a new testing phase for the guerilla force that will be of great benefit once surpassed.[42]"

On April 10, the guerillas again engaged in two ambushes, in which a total of eight Bolivian soldiers were killed, eight wounded, and 22 or 28 (the diary is unclear) taken prisoner. One of Che's men was killed[43]. On April 17, Che split up his group. Tania and another guerilla were ill and they, along with some other stragglers, were left with Joaquin (Major Juan Vitalio Acuña, a commandante in the Revolution) while Che and the remaining guerillas went off[44]. The two parties were never to meet up again.

After the discovery of the guerillas in March, American General Robert W. Porter, Chief of the Southern Command, went to Bolivia to assess the situation. Other American generals and admirals made some half dozen visits between March and Guevara's death in October. On April 18, General Porter sent Air Force Brigadier William A. Tope to Bolivia to make a full report on the guerilla situation and the help that the Bolivians needed. He stayed through April 30th, and met three times with Barrientos and also with Air Force General Ovando[45].

The Bolivian military was very weak, and both Che and the Americans knew it. General Tope, after meeting with Barrientos, wrote a report that was sent to American President Lyndon Johnson's Latin American advisor Walt Whitman Rostow. Tope reported that the Barrientos and Bolivian high command wanted fighter planes and napalm. Tope believed that the thinking of the Bolivian generals was "archaic, impulsive, and self-aggrandizing.[46]" He, like Henderson, was afraid that Barrientos would indiscriminately bomb civilians, which he believed would be counter-productive.

General Tope proposed to General Ovando that the United States train a Bolivian battalion whose mission would be to exterminate Che's guerillas[47]. Ovando was enthusiastic. As a result, on April 28, while Tope was still in Bolivia, the United States Military Advisory Group signed an agreement with the Bolivian government providing training and equipment to the Bolivian army. The entire document, entitled Memorandum of Understanding Concerning Activation, Organization and Training of the 2nd Ranger Battalion-Bolivian Army, is reproduced in the pages that follow. [**Document 22, pp. 127-129**]

The agreement opens with a recognition of a "possible threat to the internal security of the Republic of Bolivia in the Oriente," and agrees "that a rapid reaction force of battalion size capable of executing counterinsurgency operations in jungle and difficult terrain throughout this region will be created in the vicinity if Santa Cruz, Republic of Bolivia." The Bolivian Generals agreed "to furnish the troops and a suitable place to have them trained." The Americans agreed to supply and train them and provide intelligence. They promised to send sixteen American officers whose mission would be to ". . . produce a rapid reaction force capable of counter-insurgency operations."

The Americans quickly put in place the intelligence network promised in the agreement, something badly needed by the Bolivians. General Tope reported that "The Bolivians' armed forces do not have a sound, or even workable intelligence system." This was because the Bolivian army had been dismantled after the 1952 revolution and was only reconstructed beginning in 1964 with the ascendancy of the military dictatorship. Tope sent U.S. Air Force General William K. Skaer, his head of intelligence in Panama, to Bolivia to set up the network. Hector Maloney, a CIA officer, assigned to Porter's command, was also sent to help Skaer get things started[48].

On April 20, a week prior to the signing of the Memorandum of Understanding, Regis Debray and the Argentinean Ciro Bustos left the guerillas' camp along with the journalist George Andrew Roth. Roth had tracked down the guerillas and may have been a collaborator with the CIA. Debray knew nothing of this possible involvement[49]. Debray thought, wrongly, that he and Bustos could pose as journalists too. Their plan did not work, and upon walking into a village on the same day they had left Che, Debray, Bustos and Roth were captured by the Bolivian Army. Their quick capture and the fact that Roth was released in July before the others lends credibility to the assertion that Roth was indeed working with the CIA. Debray and Bustos were tortured. Debray was beaten with a hammer. Bustos confessed when shown photos of his daughters. They admitted that Che was in Bolivia, providing solid confirmation, for the first time, of what the American and Bolivian governments suspected. Bustos even provided accurate hand-drawn portraits of the guerillas. A CIA agent, a Cuban-American code-named Gabriel Garcia Garcia, aided the interrogations[50].

The summary of activity in April appearing in Che's diary is that "things are developing normally," but "we are totally cut off," "[the] peasant support base has yet to develop," and "there has not been a single new recruit." Regarding the military strategy, Che emphasizes that: "It seems certain the North Americans will intervene heavily here, having already sent helicopters and apparently the Green Berets, although they have not been seen around here." Che concludes that "morale is good among all combatants who have had their preliminary test as guerilla fighters.[51]"

On May 8, pursuant to the Memorandum of Understanding, sixteen Green Berets arrived in Bolivia to train the Bolivian Second Ranger Battalion, which had been set up to track down and eliminate the guerillas. The Green Berets had been created by President John F. Kennedy after the failure of the Americans at the Bay of Pigs, to operate as a force for international counter-insurgency. The group in Bolivia was under the leadership of an officer named Ralph "Pappy" Shelton. A career soldier, Shelton came from an impoverished family and had only a tenth-grade education. He had been wounded in Korea before going to Officers Candidate School where promising soldiers are trained to be officers. He then fought in Vietnam and Laos. Shelton arrived in Bolivia from Panama the second week of April in 1967. The training lasted until September 19th.

The Green Berets trained the Bolivians to operate in units divided into platoons, companies, and finally the battalion. They were taught how to march, shoot, detect booby traps, fight hand to hand, deal with barbed wire, and to move around at night. They built themselves up physically and practiced firing at targets. It was particularly important to teach them how to avoid ambushes. Shelton himself was reportedly very popular with local civilians. He made a point out of socializing and would visit local bars and play his guitar[52].

Meanwhile, also on May 8 Che's guerillas mounted another ambush of Bolivian soldiers, killing three and taking ten prisoners, along with some rifles, ammunition and food. The next morning they set the soldiers free[53].

On May 11, Walt Rostow wrote a letter to Johnson reporting that "the first credible report that 'Che' Guevara is alive and operating in Latin America," had been received, but that "[w]e need more evidence before concluding that Guevara is operational—and not dead. . . ." [**Document 23, p. 130**] The information probably had come from the interrogation of Bustos and Debray, or from the guerillas captured in Bolivia.

At the end of May, Che summarized his situation in his diary. Most significantly, he wrote that there now was a "total lack of contact with Manila (Havana), La Paz, and Joaquin, which reduces the group to 25.[54]" This situation was only to get worse.

CIA Agents Disguised as Bolivian Soldiers

In light of information from the interrogations of captured guerillas, and especially the information given by Debray and Bustos, the United States stepped up its efforts to implement the April agreement with the Bolivians. By mid to late June the U.S. had recruited two Cuban-Americans who would wear Bolivian military uniforms, blend in with the Bolivian soldiers and accompany the Bolivian Ranger Battalion as they sought to eliminate the guerillas. One was Gustovo Villoldo, known in Bolivia under the alias Eduardo Gonzalez.

Villoldo, a Miami counter-revolutionary who had fought in the Bay of Pigs and whose wealthy father had owned a car dealership in Havana before the revolution, was hired by the CIA to set up an intelligence network in Bolivia. Earlier in his career he had been sent by the CIA to the Congo with a group of Cuban counter-revolutionaries to help the Tshombe government to fight the Castroists who were there. He had known Che was in the Congo[55].

Villoldo first arrived in Bolivia in February, 1967, and returned there in July. In an interview in Miami on November 21, 1995, he told Jose Castaneda that "we placed a series of assets and those assets began giving us information we needed to neutralize (the uprising). That entire mechanism, that logistical support . . . left the guerillas completely isolated. We completely penetrated the urban network.[56]"

Serving under Villoldo was the second Cuban American employed by the U.S.[57]: CIA agent Felix Rodriguez, who went on to become well known as a result of his claim to be the highest ranking military officer on the scene when Che was executed. Rodriguez's 1989 autobiography is titled, with characteristic bravado, *Shadow Warrior: The CIA Hero of a Hundred Unknown Battles.* In it, he recounts how he grew up as the only child of a well-to-do provincial Cuban family of Spanish/Basque ancestry. One of his uncles was a minister in the Batista government, another was a judge. He spent time at the farm of his uncle, Feliz Mendiguitia, where he rode horses and, at the age of seven, learned to shoot a rifle. At age ten he went off to military school, living with another uncle, Jose Antonio Mendiguita, Batista's Minister of Public Works, in a big house in the expensive Miramar neighborhood in Havana. In seventh grade he left to attend a boarding school in Pennsylvania. His family opposed the July 26th Movement even before Batista's dictatorship was toppled. They moved to Miami after the revolution. Rodriguez assures his readers that they were "very much anti-communist."

At the age of 17, Rodriguez joined the Anti-Communist League of the Caribbean, sponsored by Dominican Republic strongman General Raphael Trujillo, who Rodriguez refers to as a "so-called tyrant." Thereafter, Felix trained in the Dominican Republic for an invasion of Cuba, but did not participate in the group's failed 1959 invasion. By now living in Miami, Rodriguez went on to join the Cruzada Cubana Constitutional, one of the many anti-communist groups in the city, whose goal was to "begin military operations against Castro." Rodriguez was made a platoon sergeant. He thought of himself as a "revolutionary," spoke often of "honor" and "freedom," and dreamed of "liberating Cuba." He was eighteen years old and just graduated from high school. He was given an expensive sports car by his family and spent the summer chasing girls at the beach. He decided against going to college and instead forged his father's name on an application to go to fight in Cuba.

In 1961, at the age of 21, Rodriguez volunteered to assassinate Fidel Castro with what he described as "a beautiful German bolt-action rifle with a powerful telescopic sight, all neatly packed in a custom-made padded carrying case. There was also a box of ammo, twenty rounds." A spot was picked out for the murder, at a location Castro was known to frequent. The young assassin tried three times to take a boat from Miami to Havana, but the boat failed to show up and finally the mission was cancelled. Rodriguez described himself as being "tremendously disappointed," because "I was a Cuban soldier. I considered myself at war with Fidel as I as far as I was concerned, he is still is a legitimate military target even today."

Much later, Rodriguez recounted that he had learned of many CIA attempts to murder Castro. He was asked in 1987 by the independent counsel investigating the Iran/Contra scandal if he, himself, had tried to kill Castro with an exploding cigar. "No sir, I did not," he answered. "But I did volunteer to kill that son of a bitch in 1961 with a telescopic rifle." Rodriguez participated in the Bay of Pigs invasion of the same year, where he infiltrated Cuba with a pre-invasion group. When the operation failed, he managed to evade capture and fled to Venezuela, and then back to Miami.

After his participation in the murder of Che, Rodriguez went on to work with the CIA in Vietnam and, during the Reagan-era Contra wars, in El Salvador, and Nicaragua. He boasted of his friendship with then Vice-President George Bush and proudly showed people the Rolex watch he wore as a trophy, claiming that he took it from Che after he had been killed[58].

The United States was afraid that a large presence of U.S. soldiers in Bolivia would be counter-productive and only Villoldo and Rodriguez, disguised as Bolivian army officers, were allowed to go into the combat zones. The very top levels of the American government, army, and intelligence service actively followed the unfolding events. On June 23, Rostow sent President Johnson a summary of the situation "with guerillas in Bolivia." [**Document 24, pp. 131-132**] It noted that on March 24, Bolivian security forces had been ambushed, that since then six other battles had been fought, and that the "Bolivian forces have come off badly in these engagements." Rostow's summary referred to the cable he had sent President Johnson on June 4 where he, Rostow, reported that the guerillas had between 50 and 60 people, but maybe as high as 100. He pointed out to Johnson that the seventeen-man Green Beret team had arrived and was training a new Bolivian Ranger battalion and that the CIA, because of the information given to them by Debray and Bustos, now believed Che headed the guerilla forces. At that time 600 Bolivian soldiers were in the counterinsurgency efforts, supported by the Bolivian Air Force. The plan of the Bolivian military was to maintain contact with the guerillas and block their escape until the Ranger unit being trained by the Americans could move in and eliminate them[59].

There was an urgent tone to Rostow's assessment that without U.S aid and training the problems in Bolivia might become very serious. He pointed out that the Bolivian army was "outclassed" by the guerillas, and if their forces were "augmented" the government of Bolivia could be threatened: "The outlook is not clear. The guerillas were discovered early before they were able to consolidate and take the offensive. The pursuit by the government forces, while not very effective, does keep them on the run. These are two plusses. At their present strength the guerillas do not appear to pose an immediate threat to Barrientos. If their forces were to be quickly augmented and they were able to open new fronts in the near future, as now rumored, the thin Bolivian armed forces would be hard-pressed and the fragile political situation would be threatened. The hope is that with our help Bolivian security capabilities will out-distance guerilla capabilities and eventually clear them out." [**Document 24, pp. 131-132**]

President Johnson told Rostow on June 23 to confer with the CIA, State Department, and Defense Department on the "whole guerilla problem in Latin America.[60]" The next day Rostow met with the CIA, State Department and Defense Department. Rostow put Bolivia number one on a list of the most urgent matters because of the weak army and the fragile political situation. These factors were at the center of Che's decision to go to Bolivia in the first place; evidently the CIA and State Department agreed with his analysis[61].

The United States and its Bolivian clients were moving in for the kill. Everything was in place. Rodriguez and Villoldo were on the ground providing intelligence for the Bolivian army. The head of the Bolivian Interior Ministry, Anthony Arguedos, was on the CIA's payroll, and Edward Fox of the CIA was stationed in La Paz as a "military attaché".

The American and Bolivian governments were also concerned about Che's group linking up with the Bolivian workers, particularly the militant miners at the large Silgo XX mine. In the early morning of June 24, Bolivian air force planes strafed a village housing workers from the mine and their families, killing hundreds while they were still in their beds after a celebration the previous night. This preemptive action became known as the St. John's Day Massacre[62]. The U.S. government "was complicit in the suppression of the miners.[63]" The U.S. supported MAPs (Military Assistance Programs) in the mining areas because they contributed to the "stability" of the military junta and its "reforms." The embassy in La Paz "applauded the government's response to the problem at Siglo XX." Immediately after the massacre, Rostow sent a three-page report to Johnson about the incident[64].

On June 29 William G.Bowdler, who worked for the National Security Council, was invited to meet with the Bolivian Ambassador at his residence in Washington D.C. [**Document 25, pp. 133-134**] Bowdler described most of the conversation as a "monologue by the loquacious Ambassador" about Barrientos and the political situation in Bolivia. Eventually the Bolivian ambassador got around to what was "obviously the main purpose of the invitation:" to request aid for establishing a "hunter-killer team to ferret out guerillas." The ambassador pointed out that the idea did not originate with him but came from friends of his in the CIA. Bowdler inquired whether the Ranger Battalion now in training in Bolivia was not sufficient. The ambassador replied that what he had in mind was "50 to 60 young army officers, with sufficient intelligence, motivation and drive, who could be trained quickly and could be counted on to search out the guerillas with tenacity and courage." Bowdler told him that his "idea may have merit, but needs further careful examination."[**Document 25**]

Apart from demonstrating how closely the U.S. and Bolivia cooperated in pursuing Che, this document shows how nefarious was the role of the CIA. The CIA suggests "hunter-killer" teams to Bolivian officials, and then those officials suggest them to representatives of the executive branch of the U.S. government. The United States is on both sides of the equation. Bolivia is essentially a messenger between the CIA and the National Security Council, which advises the President.

By the end of June, Che's situation was getting worse. He wrote in his diary of the "continued total lack of contact [with Joaquin's group]; and that "our most urgent task is to reestablish contact with La Paz, to replenish our military and medical supplies, and to recruit 50 to 100 men from the city." His troops were now reduced to twenty-four people[65].

In a July 5 memorandum to Rostow [**Document 26, pp. 135-136**], Bowdler summarized the current U.S. military training role in Bolivia: "DOD is helping train and equip a new Ranger Battalion. The Bolivian absorption capacity being what it is, additional military assistance would not now seem advisable. [3 lines of source text not declassified]"

On that same July 5, a high-level meeting was held at the White House. Rostow, Bowdler, and Peter Jessup (another National Security Council staffer) met in the Situation Room with representatives of the Department of State, Henderson, the Ambassador to Bolivia, a Department of Defense official, and two CIA officials, Desmond FitzGerald and William Broe. The group agreed that the special strike force that had been requested by Bolivia at the suggestion of the CIA was not advisable because of the U.S. Embassy's objections. They decided that the United States should "concentrate on the training of the Second Ranger Battalion with the preparation of an intelligence unit to be part of the Battalion." [**Document 26**]

They summarized the "U.S. efforts to support the counterinsurgency program in Bolivia against Cuban-led guerillas," stating that it "should follow a two-step approach." Alongside the 16-man military training team from the U.S. Special Forces, the United States should also provide "ammunition, radios, and communications equipment on an emergency basis under MAP and expedited delivery of four helicopters." [**Document 26**]

Intelligence was also a concern, and here the CIA was given primary responsibility: "As the training of the Ranger battalion progressed, weaknesses in its intelligence-collecting capability emerged. The CIA was formally given responsibility for developing a plan to provide such a capability on July 14th. . . . A team of two instructors arrived in La Paz on August 2. In addition to training the Bolivians in intelligence-collection techniques, the instructors [text not declassified] planned to accompany the Second Ranger battalion into the field. Although the team was assigned in an advisory capacity, the CIA 'expected that they will actually help in directing operations.' The Agency also regarded this plan 'as a pilot program for probable duplication in other Latin American countries faced with the problem of guerilla warfare.'" [**Document 26**] The two instructors, as we have seen, were Villoldo and Rodriguez.

A Department of Defense Intelligence Information Report dated August 11, 1967, describes "the first organized operation conducted by the Bolivian Army in the current guerilla situation," during the period July 8-27. [**Document 27, pp. 137-139**] The two page report was likely transmitted by the CIA agents on the ground in Bolivia—either Rodriguez or Villoldo—but as the names of the sources, the originators, the references, and the approving author were blacked out, we do not know who prepared it. It is accompanied by a map showing the area near Nacahuazu where hundreds of the Bolivian rangers had carried out military sweeps. The operation was considered a success by the Americans accompanying them, "even though they were not successful in capturing a guerilla unit." One guerilla was reportedly killed. On July 9, after the first encounter with the guerillas, an abandoned encampment was located, and a piece of paper found in an empty toothpaste tube listed 11 names: JOAQUIN, POLO, PEDRO, ALEJANDRO, MEDICO, TANIA, VICTOR, WALTER, BRAULO, NEGRO and GUEVARA. The operation supposedly enhanced the morale of the Rangers and "for the first time, upon being fired upon, they did not drop their weapons and run."

At the end of July, Che reports in his diary that the "total lack of contact [with Joaquin's group] continues." He writes that we have 22 men, with three disabled (including me), which decreases our mobility.[66]"

In early August, the Bolivian army, aided by detailed maps that Bustos had drawn for them, found the storage caves and the old base camp at Nancahuazu. Che wrote in his diary on August 14 that it was a "bad day," and that "this was the worst blow they have delivered." Documentation in the caves led the Bolivians to Loyola Guzman, the key contact and financial organizer of the support network in La Paz. She attempted suicide by throwing herself from an upper story of the Ministry of Government building, but survived. Documents found in the caves were sent to CIA headquarters in Langley, Virginia, for analysis. Rostow wrote a note to Johnson about the find, telling him that the Bolivians wanted all the materials back to use as evidence in the upcoming trial against Debray[67].

The Net Closes

On August 28, Joaquin, Tania, and eight others were ambushed crossing the Masicuri River and all but one were killed. [**Document 28, pp. 140-142**]. Joaquin's group was betrayed to the Bolivian army by a farmer named Honorato Rojas. According to Jose Castillo Chavez, a Bolivian guerilla survivor whose *nom de guerre* was Paco, Rojas was bribed—with an offer of money and the possibility of taking his whole family to the United States—by a CIA agent in Santa Cruz named Irving Ross. It was Rojas who told the Bolivians where the group was going to make a crossing and the army laid in wait. Che had lost one-third of his troop. Barrientos attended Tania's burial in Vallegrande a week later when her body was recovered in the river. The remaining guerillas were now caught in a vise between two Bolivian divisions. Rostow wrote to Johnson that the "Bolivian armed forces finally scored their first victory—and it seems to have been a big one.[68]" He told Johnson that the Second Ranger Battalion would be going into operation soon after[69].

On or about August 31 Felix Rodriguez, at least as he tells it, interrogated Paco, the survivor of the massacre of Joaquin's group. Paco identified the people in Che's band and, Rodriguez claims, provided information that allowed him to calculate Che's exact location. Paco supposedly told him that a guerilla named Miguel who led a vanguard was always 1,000 meters in advance of the main troop led by Che. When Miguel was killed in September, Rodriquez claims to have identified him by his fingerprints and thereby knew exactly where Che was. Although their training had yet to be completed, the Second Ranger Battalion departed immediately for the guerilla zone, hastened by the information Rodriguez had garnered[70].

Che's diary at the end of August concluded that "Without doubt this was the worst month we have had in this war. The loss of all the caves with the documents and medicines was a heavy blow, psychologically above all else. The loss of two men at the end of the month and the subsequent march on only horsemeat demoralized the troops, and sparked the first case of desertion . . . The lack of contact with the outside and with Joaquin, and the fact that prisoners taken from his group talked, also demoralized the troops somewhat. My illness sowed uncertainty among several others and all this was reflected in our only clash . . ."

Che listed the most important issues facing the group as a lack of "contact of any kind; no reasonable hope of establishing it in the near future," no ability "to recruit peasants," and "a decline in combat morale; temporary, I hope.[71]"

September was a month of some skirmishes, news about the loss of Tania and the others, and what Che labels "Defeat" near the town of La Higuera[72]. On September 26 Coco (Peredo), Miguel (Hernandez) and Julio (Gutierrez) were killed. Peredo, a Bolivian guerilla leader, was one of Che's most important men. Rodriguez urged the Bolivians to move the Ranger battalion headquarters to Vallegrande which is near La Higuera[73]. On September 29, again according to Rodriguez, the Bolivians were persuaded to move the 2nd Ranger battalion to Vallegrande. Rodriguez joined these six hundred and fifty men who had been "so well trained" by U.S. Special Forces Major "Pappy" Shelton[74].

By the end of September Che reported that, after an ambush in which some of his men were killed, they were in a "perilous position." He also wrote that "there may be truth to the various reports about fatalities in the other [Joaquin's] group, so we must consider them wiped out. . . . The features are the same as last month, except that now the army is demonstrating more effectiveness in action and the peasant masses are not helping us with anything and are becoming informers . . . The most important task is to escape and seek more favorable areas . . ." This was not to be[75].

Che's last diary entry is for October 7. On that date, the 17 remaining members of the troop were in a ravine near La Higuera[76]. Che notes that "the 11 month anniversary of our establishment as a guerilla force passed in a bucolic mood with no complications . . ." The troop met an old woman named Epifania tending her goats about one league from Higueras and went to her house. They gave her and her daughters 50 pesos with "instructions to not say a word, but we have little hope she will stick to her promise.[77]" The old woman never did betray Che, and went to the mountains with her two daughters out of fear of the army. But someone else did inform on them: A local peasant, Pedro Pena, saw the guerillas pass his potato field, and the army was tipped off[78].

In his introduction to Che's *Bolivian Diary*, Fidel Castro wrote of the events of the next day, October 8, 1967. "On October 7 Che wrote his last lines. The following day, at 1:00 p.m., in the narrow ravine where he proposed waiting until nightfall in order to break out of the encirclement, a large enemy force made contact with them. The small group of men who now made up the detachment fought heroically until dusk. From individual positions located on the bottom of the ravine, and on the cliffs above, they faced a mass of soldiers who surrounded and attacked them[79] . . ."

Che was captured in the early afternoon on October 8 by Captain Gary Prado of the Bolivian Second Ranger Battalion. He had been wounded in the leg and was weaponless. His rifle had been shot out from under him. Together with his comrade Willy he was escorted to the village of La Higuera where he was held in a tiny schoolhouse.

Meanwhile, Back in Washington . . .

On October 9 a Department of State Telegram from American Ambassador Henderson in La Paz to the Secretary of State in Washington D.C. stated that, the previous day, Che Guevara had been wounded in the leg and taken prisoner by Bolivian Army units in Higueras on Sunday. [**Document 29, p. 143**] The telegram states that Che had been wounded in the leg but was alive. It calls this information reliable, presumably because it came from the CIA agents who were there. The key portion reads as follows:

"SUBJECT: CHE GUEVARA

[The document is in all capitals but is transcribed here in upper and lower case]

1: According [BLOCKED] Che Guevara taken prisoner by Bolivian Army units in Higueras area southwest of Villagrande Sunday, October 8.

2: Guevara reliably reported still alive with leg wound in custody of Bolivian troops in Higueras morning October 9."

Contradicting this document, however, is another sent to President Johnson and excerpted below, in which President Barrientos is quoted as saying that by 10 a.m. on October 9, Che was already dead. In fact, Che was not murdered until after 1 p.m. on the following day.

At 6:10 p.m. on October 9, Walter Rostow wrote a Memorandum to President Johnson on White House stationery that the Bolivians "got" Che Guevara, qualifying this by saying it was unconfirmed. [**Document 30, p. 144**] Rostow writes that the Bolivian unit responsible for this is "the one we have been training for some time and has just entered the field of action." The Rostow

Memorandum cites information given by President Barrientos to newsmen at 10 a.m. on October 9 (although not for publication), that "Che Guevara is dead." It further states that the "Bolivian armed forces believes Rangers have surrounded guerilla force boxed into canyon and expect to eliminate them soon."

On October 10 Bowdler of the National Security Council Staff sent a note to Rostow on White House stationery that there is "no firm reading on whether Che Guevara was among the casualties of the October 8 engagement." [**Document 31, p.145**] This statement is quite remarkable, as Che had been murdered the day before, with the CIA agent Felix Rodriguez present. So the CIA certainly was aware of Guevara's murder. However, it appears that Bowdler and the National Security Council were out of the loop, probably intentionally.

The next document dated October 11 at 10:30 a.m. from Rostow to President Johnson is central to the claim, including that made by Castaneda, that the United States did not want Che executed. In the document Rostow calls the killing "stupid" with its implication that the U.S. was not involved. [**Document 32, pp. 146-147**] However, on examination, the document is self-serving, and it proves nothing of the sort. In fact, its substance can be read as to the contrary. It lays out all of the reasons why the U.S. government would want Che executed and claims 99% certainty that this has been achieved. It then leaves a blank for something that is to arrive in Washington within a day. The omitted sentence most likely refers to Che's fingerprints, or even possibly his hands (cut off from his corpse in Bolivia), that were being sent to Washington to verify his identity.

The Memorandum then gives a cover story that attempts to hide the U.S. role in the murder. It details what the CIA told the National Security Council concerning the murder which it claims was ordered by the head of the Bolivian Armed Forces:

"CIA tells us that the latest information is that Guevara was taken alive. After a short interrogation to establish his identity, General Ovando—Chief of the Bolivian Armed Forces—ordered him shot. I regard this as stupid, but it is understandable from a Bolivian standpoint, given the problems which the sparing of French communist and Castro courier Regis Debray has caused them."

General Ovando may or may not have ordered Che murdered, but it is unlikely he did so without instructions from, or in agreement with, U.S. officials, inasmuch as the U.S. had paid for the entire Bolivian operation; and the U.S. military and CIA personnel had trained, accompanied, and directed the "hunter-killer" groups whose job it was to "eliminate" the guerillas. Felix Rodriguez's story, if true, also makes it doubtful that the U.S wanted Che kept alive. Rodriguez, posing as a Bolivian officer, claims he was the highest military officer on the scene when the murder occurred. Would he have transmitted an order to murder Che had such an order been contrary to the wishes of his CIA employer? To ask the question is to answer it.

Moreover, why should we believe what the CIA told Rostow? It seems very likely that Rostow was misled to give him, the President, and the State Department plausible deniability. The execution without trial of a captured combatant of any sort, guerilla or soldier, is a war crime. Taking responsibility for the murder of Che might also have made relationships with Latin America more difficult. Blaming the murder on Bolivia provided cover for a U.S. /CIA operation. From the documents mentioned earlier there is evidence that the CIA did not always fully share information with the National Security Council. As we have seen above, the documents show that Rostow reported that Che was dead when he had not yet been murdered, a fact known to the CIA, and that Bowdler, on October 10, wrote to Rostow that there was no evidence to support a conclusion that Che was dead at a time when the CIA knew he was. Since 1948, the CIA has engaged in illegal actions that it does not reveal directly to the Executive so that the President can deny an accusation with plausibility.

But whether or not Rostow was told the truth by the CIA is beside the point. For despite his statement indicating that he regarded it as "stupid" to murder Che, the substance of his memorandum to President Johnson is that Che's death benefits U.S. policy. His claim that somehow Che should not have been killed is undercut, to say the least, by the benefits he sees in Che's death. Here is the key part of the memorandum to President Johnson where Rostow outlines the importance of Che's death:

"The death of Guevara carries these significant implications:

— It marks the passing of another of the aggressive, romantic revolutionaries like Sukarno, Nkrumah, Ben Bella—and reinforces this trend.

— In the Latin American context, it will have a strong impact in discouraging would-be guerillas.

—It shows the soundness of our "preventive medicine" assistance to countries facing incipient insurgency—it was the Bolivian 2nd Ranger battalion, trained by our Green Berets from June-September of this year that cornered him and got him.

We have put these points across to several newsmen."

As Rostow points out, Che's death can now be added to the list of deaths of other "romantic revolutionaries," and that it will discourage other guerillas. In other words, while there would have been some benefits to U.S. counterinsurgency policy just from Che's capture, these were much stronger as a result of his death. There is simply no way that the United States government, including Rostow, wanted Che kept alive. It was against what they perceived as their best interests. They thought his death was a major blow to revolutionary movements and wanted the press to know it.

A day after Rostow summarized the positives of Che's death for the United States government and Latin America, the Director of Intelligence and Research at the State Department wrote a six-page report entitled "Guevara's Death—the Meaning for Latin America." [**Document 33, pp. 148-151**] The report dated October 12, 1967 went to Rostow and the National Security Council. It emphasized, in even stronger terms than had Rostow, the positive importance of Che's death:

"Che" Guevara's death was a crippling—perhaps fatal—blow to the Bolivian guerilla movement and may prove a serious setback for Fidel Castro's hopes to foment violent revolution in 'all or almost all' Latin American countries. Those Communists and others who might have been prepared to initiate Cuban-style guerilla warfare will be discouraged, at least for a time, by the defeat of the foremost tactician of the Cuban revolutionary strategy at the hands of one of the weakest armies in the hemisphere."

It continues by measuring the effects of Che's death in Bolivia:

"Effects in Bolivia. Guevara's death is a feather in the cap of Bolivian President Rene Barrientos. It may signal the end of the guerilla movement as a threat to stability."

And then in Latin America:

"Probable Latin American reaction to Guevara's death. News of Guevara's death will relieve most non-leftist Latin Americans who feared that sooner or later he might foment insurgencies in their countries."

And finally, it assents that the death will strengthen the peaceful line of the Latin American communist parties affiliated with Moscow:

"If the Bolivian guerilla movement is soon eliminated as a serious subversive threat, the death of Guevara will have even more important repercussions among Latin American communists. The dominant peaceful line groups, who were either in total disagreement with Castro or paid only lip-service to the guerilla struggle, will be able to argue with more authority against the Castro-Guevara-Debray thesis. They can point out that even a movement led by the foremost revolutionary tactician, in a country which apparently provided conditions suitable for revolution, had failed."

In a very short note to President Johnson, dated October 13 at 4:00 p.m., and written on White House stationery, Rostow writes: "This removes any doubt that 'Che' Guevara is dead." [**Document 34, p. 152**] The "this" referred to is blanked out of the note, but as is clear from other documents, the fingerprints from Che's cut-off hands have been matched with prior copies of Che's fingerprints.

Rodriguez's Inconsistencies

The next document is also dated October 13 and is from the Director of the CIA, Richard Helms, to Rostow, the Secretary of State, and the Secretary of Defense. [**Document 35, pp. 153-155**] The subject is described as "Statements by Ernesto 'Che' Guevara Prior to His Execution in Bolivia." Although the source of the information is excised, the context makes clear that CIA operative Felix Rodriguez supplied the content. This does not make the content true, but it is the earliest full statement we have on the record from Rodriguez. The document makes interesting reading, although again we do not know how much is accurate. According to Rodriguez he got access to Che on October 9 at around 7 a.m. Che "was sitting on the floor in the corner of a small, dark schoolroom, in Higueras. He had his hands over his face. His wrists and feet were tied." Che refused to be interrogated but "permitted himself to be drawn into a conversation." According to Rodriguez, Che discussed the Cuban economic situation, Camilo Cienfuegos, Fidel, the Congo, treatment of guerilla prisoners in Cuba, and the future of the guerilla movement.

He wrote further that "a telegraphic code was arranged between La Paz and Higueras with the number 500 representing Guevara, 600 meaning the phrase 'keep alive' and 700 representing 'execute.'" The order to execute came at 11:50 a.m. from La Paz and Guevara was executed with "a burst of shots at 1:15 p.m.

According to this document, Che's last words were: "Tell my wife to remarry and tell Fidel Castro that the Revolution will again rise in the Americas." To his frightened and hesitant executioner he said, "Remember, you are killing a man." Rodriguez states that "it was impossible to keep him alive."

Rodriguez was again debriefed about Che's execution almost ten years later. [**Document 40, pp. 179-184**] The interview, on May 29, 1975, by the Deputy Inspector of the CIA, was likely pursuant to the Church Committee hearings (United States Senate Select Committee to Study Governmental Operations with Respect to Intelligence Activities). In this interview, Rodriguez took credit for just about everything with regard to the capture and killing of Che. He claimed that it was he who insured the Bolivian 2nd Ranger Battalion was deployed immediately to Vallegrande when it appeared Guevara was likely to be in that area. He claims that when he and Villoldo were given instructions about their mission in Bolivia "there was a clear one [instruction] that in the event the Bolivian Army captured Guevara they should do everything possible 'to keep him alive.'" He says that, when Guevara was captured, he sent a message to the U.S. asking that an Embassy representative be sent to the area to prevail upon the Bolivians to spare Che's life as he did not think he could succeed in doing so. Even if he sent such a message, which he might have as cover for the murder to follow, no Embassy representative ever appeared. He then claims, as he did in the earlier briefing, that as the highest ranking "Bolivian officer" he received the call to execute Che on the military field telephone. This time, he says he was given the code numbers "500 and 600."

"He said he knew that 500 referred to Guevara, 600 to the word execute and 700 to the preservation of Guevara's life. These simple codes had been identified to him previously."

As we noted earlier, in the 1967 summary of his report on the execution Rodriguez had said that "600" meant "keep alive" and "700" meant "execute." [**Document 35, pp. 153-155**] That he was mixed up about "these simple codes" concerning the most important moment in his life, raises questions about his claims that it was he who received the call, transmitted the order, and could do nothing to stop the murder. Rodriguez said he "was left with the implementation of the execution." He "told a sergeant of the order to execute Guevara and entrusted the mission to him."

The CIA interviewer is evidently skeptical about Rodriguez's claim that he received the order to execute Guevara from higher ranking Bolivian officers.

After all, the CIA agents (Rodriguez and Villoldo) had never before given orders by Bolivian officers. According to the Deputy Inspector General:

"Despite their apparent status as Bolivian officers, [Rodriguez] said that they never were given orders by higher-ranking Bolivian officers. (One exception to this rule was the order which Colonel [   ] issued to [Rodriguez] on the day of Guevara's execution if [Rodriguez's] story is to be believed)."

Rodriguez repeatedly says he was ordered to keep Che alive if captured, that he wanted Che kept alive, and there was nothing he could do to stop the execution. This was standard operating procedure for the CIA, as we have seen: U.S. fingerprints were not to be found on any of the assassinations carried out during this period. Plausible deniability was of key importance to the U.S. and especially the President and Department of State. Rodriguez's story and the other stories of Che's murder gave the U.S. that deniability. In the context of the Church committee, which was investigating the CIA and Presidentially ordered assassinations, this deniability was important.

The Bolivian Death Documents

On October 16, 1967, the High Command of the Bolivian Armed Forces released a statement regarding the death of Che Guevara. The statement is contained in a Department of State Airgram dated October 18, 1967, from the Embassy at La Paz to various U.S. officials. [**Document 37, pp. 158-163**] Attached to the Airgram are four annexes including the Death Certificate, the Autopsy Report, the Argentine Police Report and a Communiqué from the Argentine Embassy. Argentina had cooperated by sending fingerprint and handwriting experts as it had a copy of Che's prints in his Argentine identity records. The experts confirmed a fingerprint match as well as a match of Che's handwriting with that in his *Diary*.

The statement issued by the high command even as late as October 16th is of interest because, in it, the Bolivians still claimed Che died as a result of battle wounds:

"[C]oncerning the combat that took place at La Higuera between units of the Armed forces and the red group commanded by Ernesto "Che" Guevara, as a result of which he, among others, lost his life, the following is established:

"Ernesto Guevara fell into the hands of our troops gravely wounded and in full use of his mental faculties. After the combat ended, he was transferred to the town of La Higuera, more or less at 8 p.m. on Sunday, October 8, where he died as a result of his wounds. His body was transferred to the city of Vallegrande at 4 p.m. on Monday, October 9, in a helicopter of the Bolivian Air Force."

American Ambassador Henderson, in a classified comment, was critical of the Bolivian claims, and wrote that the Bolivian statement did not answer questions about Che's death:

"BEGIN CLASSIFIED. . . . "The documents do little, however, to resolve public speculation on the timing and manner of death. It will be widely noted that neither the death certificate nor the autopsy report state a time of death. . . . This would appear to be an attempt to bridge the difference between a series of earlier divergent statements from Armed Forces sources, ranging from assertions that he died during or shortly after battle to those suggesting he survived at least twenty-four hours. Some early reports last week also indicated that Guevara was captured with minor injuries while later statements, including the attached autopsy report, affirm that he suffered multiple and serious bullet wounds.

We doubt that the communiqué will satisfactorily answer these questions and are inclined to agree with the comment by <u>Presencia</u> columnist <u>Politicus</u> that these discrepancies, now that the identity of the body is generally accepted, are 'going to be the new focus of polemics in the coming days, especially abroad.' END CLASSIFIED."

It is surprising that Henderson appears so out of touch with what really occurred. By October 16th Rodriguez had transmitted his version of events to the CIA, which knew that Che had been executed. [**Document 35, pp. 153-155**] This is again an indication that Henderson, and possibly others at State, may have been kept in the dark, at least for a while, about the murder. This would allow them to deny involvement in a CIA killing operation.

A Department of Defense document dated November 28, 1967, gives the results of a debriefing of the officers of the 2nd Ranger Battalion's activities from September 26 to October 31, and the details concerning the execution of "Che" Guevara. [**Document 38, pp. 164-173**] In an earlier version issued as a Department of Defense Intelligence Information Report dated November 9, 1967, the names of the Bolivians are excised, but they are included in the November 28 document. The document describes in detail the various battles in late September and October that led to Che's wounding and capture as well as the efforts to eliminate the remainder of Che's guerillas after his capture. Attached to the document are four hand-drawn maps of the key battles. [**Document 39, pp. 174-178**]

A section of the report consists of an interview on October 30, 1967, with Lt. Espinoza Lord of Company B, 2nd Ranger Battalion, regarding the handling of Che after his capture.

"Lt. Espinoza talked at length with Guevara, though Guevara did not reveal any pertinent information. Early in the morning of the 9th of October, the unit received the order to execute Guevara and the other captives. . . . The Officers involved did not know where the order originated, but felt that it came from the highest echelons. Cpt. Prado gave the order to execute Guevara to Lt. Perez, but he was unable to carry out the order and in turn gave it to Sgt. Terran), Company B. . . . By this time, Sgt. Terran had fortified his courage with several beers and returned to the room where Guevara was being held prisoner. When Terran entered the room, Guevara stood up, hands tied in front, and stated, "I know what you have come for. I am ready." Terran looked at him for a few minutes and then said, "No you are mistaken, be seated." Sgt. Terran then left the room for a few moments.

Sgt. Terran returned to the room where Guevara was being held. When he entered, Guevara stood and faced him. Sgt. Terran told Guevara to be seated but he refused to sit down and stated "I will remain standing for this." The Sgt. began to get angry and told him to be seated again, but Guevara would say nothing. Finally Guevara told him, "Know this, you are killing a man." Terran then fired a burst from his M2 Carbine, knocking Guevara back into the wall of the small house."

Espinoza does not make any mention of Rodriguez (Ramos) and states that the order to execute Che came in the early morning whereas Rodriguez says it came almost at noon. [**Document 35, pp. 153-155**] This discrepancy is simply another indication that there are differing stories about the facts of Che's murder and that Rodriguez's assertions are untrustworthy. Recall also that, in addition to Espinoza's statement, which does not mention Rodriguez, there are the notes of Bolivian Colonel Selich that John Lee Anderson reviewed. Again, there is no mention made of any order being transmitted to or from Rodriguez.

Rodriguez's diversion of blame away from the CIA has been a longstanding accomplishment. But his story is wholly discredited by the documentary facts and historical circumstances. The CIA has been a paramilitary organization since 1948, a year after its creation. It can and does function with a certain autonomy, so much so that a 1975 commission of the U.S. Senate was set up to investigate its practice of political assassinations. As the historian of U.S. anti-communist foreign policy and ex-foreign service officer William Blum sets out in his book, *Killing Hope*, from 1948 until 1967, the year of Che's murder, a documented nineteen prominent foreign individual assassinations (or planning for same) were carried out by the agency[80].

In addition to those documents reproduced in this book, there are likely to be others that are still unavailable to us. Those documents would likely deal with communications between the CIA and the Department of State, and the Bolivian generals and the Bolivian President after Che's capture. But, to summarize from the documents we do have, the record shows that: The CIA had been keeping track of Che since 1954, five years before the Cuban revolution, when he was a young doctor in Guatemala. After the revolution, they regularly documented his whereabouts and activities. The CIA, acting through Chicago mobster Johnny Rosselli, had previously tried to kill Che by poison in Cuba. Most damning in our recounting is the prior understanding the CIA country chief Gustavo Villoldo admits to having arrived at with General Rene Barrientos where they agreed that if Che were captured he was to be killed. Barrientos gave Villoldo his "word as President of Bolivia" that this would be done. When Che was killed, counterinsurgency head Walt Rostow crowed over the murder pointing out to Johnson the good this would do for the U.S. The CIA followed suit in its assessment of what Che's death meant for the prospects of revolution in Latin America. The autonomy from the legislative and the executive that the CIA enjoyed was necessitated by the practice of "plausible deniability," an Orwellian formulation for lying. That practice allowed the CIA and the President to claim they had clean hands. As George Orwell wrote in 1984, "Who controls the past controls the future. Who controls the present controls the past."

Fidel's Eulogy

On October 19, 1967, a mass public ceremony to honor Che was held in Havana's Plaza de la Revolution. After the showing of film clips of Che and

Fidel and a 21-gun salute, Fidel delivered a moving eulogy. Speaking of Che's heroic victories, Fidel acknowledged that the death of Che "is a hard blow, it is a tremendous blow to the revolutionary movement because, without any doubt it deprives it of its most experienced and capable chief."

"However, how must revolutionaries face this adverse blow? How must they face this loss? What would be Che's opinion if he had to make a judgment on this subject? He expressed that opinion very clearly when he wrote in his message to the Latin American Solidarity Organization that if death surprised him at any place, it would be welcome, providing that his battle cry had reached a receptive ear and another hand was stretched out to grasp a weapon. And that was his battle cry. It will not reach one receptive ear, but millions of receptive ears, not one hand, but millions of hands outstretching to grasp weapons, inspired by his example."

On July 13, 1997, "the remains of Latin American revolutionary hero Che Guevara, buried since 1967 in an unmarked grave in rural Bolivia, were returned to Cuba.' [**Document 43, pp. 198-199**]

Che's Legacy

While today there are few if any Guevarist organizations leading armed struggle in the countryside, Che's struggle for a better world lives on. Che now symbolizes "a certain *spirit,* both ethical and political, formed from revolt against the domination of imperialism, rage against capitalist social injustices, intransigent struggle against the established order, and the intense desire for a socialist revolutionary transformation of society.[81]"

Nowhere was this shown to be more true than in Bolivia, with the 2005 election of its first indigenous president Evo Morales. In his inauguration speech Morales paid homage to Che Guevara, "who fought for a new world of equality.[82]" In the Morales government are militants, like Loyola Guzman, who fought along Che in the Bolivian ELN (*Ejercito de Liberation Nacional de Bolivia.*) When Morales was asked to address the question: "Why do I like Che?" he responded: "I like Che because he fought for equality, for justice. He did not just care for ordinary people; he made their struggle his own.[83]"

When interviewed about Che in 2006, Fidel reflected: "What did he leave behind? I believe the biggest thing is, really, his moral values, his conscience. Che symbolized the highest human values, and he was an extraordinary example. He created a great aura, a great mystique. I admired him a great deal, and loved him.[84]"

Che left behind the legend of a man who died for acting on his ideas, not just talking about them. Che embodied the hope of succeeding generations that the world can and must be changed, in the words of Che's African-American contemporary Malcolm X, "by any means necessary."

"They guillotined Charlotte Corday and they said Marat is dead. No Marat is not dead. Put him in the Pantheon or throw him in the sewer; it doesn't matter—he's back the next day. He's reborn in the man who has no job, the woman who has no bread, in the girl who has to sell her body, in the child who hasn't learned to read; he's reborn in the unheated tenement, in the wretched mattress without blankets, in the unemployed, in the proletariat, in the brothel, in the jailhouse, in your laws that show no pity, in your schools that give no future, and he appears in all that is ignorance and he recreates himself from all that is darkness. Oh, beware human society: you cannot kill Marat until you have killed the misery of poverty." —Victor Hugo

Viva Che!

Notes

1. Michael J. Hogan, *A Cross of Iron: Harry S. Truman and the Origins of the National Security State, 1945-1954*. New York: Cambridge University Press, 1998, p.65
2. Peter Grosse, *Gentleman Spy: The Life of Allen Dulles*. New York: Houghton Mifflin, 1994, p. 293
3. Ibid.
4. James W. Douglas, *JFK and the Unspeakable: Why He Died & Why It Matters*. Orbis Books, 2008, p. 33
5. Ibid., p.33
6. *Alleged Assassination Plots Involving Foreign Leaders: An Interim Report*, (also known as the Church Committee, after Senator Frank Church, its convener), November 20, 1975 Washington; U.S. Government Printing Office, 1975, p.151, Ibid., as quoted in Douglas, Ibid., p. 34
7. Ibid., p. 150
8. Rodriguez, p. 160
9. Rodriguez, pp. 160-164
10. Castaneda, p. 401
11. Ibid., p. 402
12. Ibid., p. 402
13. Castaneda, p. 403; Gustavo Villoldo, interview with the author, Miami, November 27, 1995; endnote 14 in Chapter 11, page 444
14. Taibo, p. 556
15. Taibo, p. 556
16. Ryan, p. 132
17. Ryan, p. 132
18. Harris, pp. 219-221
19. See also *Alleged Assassination Plots*, pp.74-77
20. Ibid.
21. Jon Lee Anderson, *Che: A Revolutionary Life*. New York: Grove Press, p. 45
22. Anderson, p. 48
23. Anderson, pp. 72-94
24. *Notas del Segundo Diario de viaje*, 1955
25. Anderson, p. 211
26. Anderson, p.310
27. Anderson, p. 387
28. See *Superpower Principles: U.S. Terrorism Against Cuba*, edited by Salim Lamrani, Common Courage Press, 2005, p. 139

29. Anderson, p. 449
30. *Che Guevara and the FBI,* pp. 174, 180
31. Anderson, p. 628
32. William Blum,· *Killing Hope: US Military and CIA Interventions Since World War II,* chapter 26
33. Fidel reading the letter and a translation into English can be found at http://www. embacubalebanon.com/chelettere.html and in *Che Guevara and the FBI,* p. 134.
34. Norman Gall, *Slow Death in Bolivia,* http://www.normangall.com/bolivia_art1.htm
35. Fidel Castro and Ignacio Ramonet, *Fidel Castro: My Life,* New York:Scribner, 2008, p. 301
36. *Bolivian Diary,* Analysis of the Month, p. 44
37. *Bolivian Diary,* Analysis of the Month, p. 60
38. *Bolivian Diary,* Analysis of the Month, p. 78
39. *Bolivian Diary,* Analysis of the Month pp. 94-5
40. *Bolivian Diary,* March 27, 1967, p. 113
41. *Bolivian Diary* March 23, 1967, p. 111
42. *Bolivian Diary,* Analysis of the Month, p. 118
43. *Bolivian Diary,* April 10, 1967, p. 126
44. *Bolivian Diary,* April 17, 1967, p. 132
45. Ryan, p. 83
46. Ryan, p. 85
47. Ryan, p. 85
48. Ryan, pp. 95–6
49. http://www.leandrokatz.com/Pages/ChronoEnglCheFour.html
50. Anderson, p. 718
51. *Bolivian Diary,* Summary of the month, pp. 143-45
52. Ryan, p.94
53. *Bolivian Diary,* May 8-9, 1967, p. 149
54. *Bolivian Diary,* Summary of the month, pp. 163-64
55. Castaneda, p. 312
56. Ibid., p. 367
57. Ryan, p. 96
58. Luciak, Ilja A., *After the Revolution,* p. 30
59. Ryan, p.81
60. Ryan, p. 80
61. Ryan, p. 64
62. James D. Cockcroft, *Neighbors in Turmoil,* New York: Harper and Row, p. 429
63. Ibid., Ryan p. 100
64. Ryan, p. l00
65. *Bolivian Diary,* Analysis of the Month, p.182
66. *Bolivian Diary,* Analysis of the month p. 191
67. Ryan, pp. 115-117

68. Ryan, p. 121
69. LBJ libr., NSF, Country File: Bolivia, vol. 4, box 8, doc. 106
70. Rodriguez, pp. 155-56
71. *Bolivian Diary*, August, Summary of the Month pp. 221-222
72. *Bolivian Diary*, September 26, p. 242
73. Rodriguez, p. 155
74. Rodriguez, p. 156
75. *Bolivian Diary*, pp. 247-8
76. Anderson, p. 732
77. *Bolivian Diary*, October 7, p. 253
78. Gary Prado Salmon, *The Defeat of Che Guevara*, p. 174
79. Fidel Castro's, *A Necessary Introduction, The Bolivian Diary* , p. 28
80. Blum, Ibid, p.453 for entire list through 1991, which includes 33 persons in various parts of the world.
81. Olivier Besancenot and Michel Lowy, *CHE GUEVARA: His Revolutionary Legacy*, Monthly Review Press, New York, NY, 2009, p. 82
82. Ibid, p. 82
83. Rieff, David, *Che's Second Coming? The New York Times*, Nov. 20, 2005

DOCUMENTS

#261 746

BIO DATA

NAME: GUEVARA de la Serna, Ernesto
             aka Che

DPOB: 14 June 1928, Rosario, Argentina

TRAVEL: Visited United States August 1952.

FATHER: GUEVARA Lynch, Ernesto

Document 1. Che Guevara's passport and "Bio Data" (1952)
1952: The first document in Che Guevara's file is a copy of his Argentine passport and
tourist visa. Information was entered on a separate "Bio Data" sheet.

GUEVARA, Ernesto

ARGENTINA
a/o July 1956

LOMBARDO TOLEDANO PROTEGE—Ernesto Guevara, an Argentine Communist recently arrested in Mexico in connection with the Fidel Castro plot against President Batista of Cuba, enjoys two official sinecures in Mexico, "one as a doctor at General Hospital, although he has never studied medicine," for which he receives 1,500 pesos a month, and another as a teacher in the School of Medicine at the University, for which he is paid 800 pesos a month. At present he is still under arrest, with Dr. Fidel Castro. Nevertheless he continues to receive his salaries. Upon his arrival in Mexico City, after he was expelled from Guatemala following the fall of the Arbenz Government, Guevara became a protege of Vicente Lombardo Toledano, who accepted him as an active member of the Partido Popular, and it was Lombardo Toledano who obtained the two sinecures for him. (Mexico, D.F., CGV Agency, July 25, 1956, 1500 GMT—E)

Cárdena García Velbao Agency

FBIS Rept., July 26, 1956   OFF. USE ONLY

Document 2. File card on Che Guevara (July 1956)
1956: File card with information about Che Guevara shortly after his arrest on June 24, 1956, in Mexico as a member of the group led by Fidel Castro planning an invasion of Cuba. Contains erroneous information such as "never studied medicine." Typical of the file cards kept by U.S. spy agencies on any potential "troublemakers."

GUEVARA SERNA, Ernesto   Argentina

    On July 2, Hilda Gadea de Guevara denied that she or Ernesto

Guevara Serna, Her Argentine physician husband, are communists. She
was forced to leave Peru, she stated, not for Communist activities,
but because she was statistical decretary of;the APRA; neither she nor
her husband have everh had Communist sympathies. She further denied
the rumor that she and her husband had come to Mexico from Gustemala
with Rogelio Cruz Wer and Jaime Rosenbery, chiefs of the Civil Guard
and the Judicial Guard under the Arbenz regime, respectively.
She stated that neither she nor her husband knew either of these men
when they were in Guatemala.
Mexico City Excelsior, 3 July 56.

SO:CIA, FOreign Documentary Summary, # 1017, 30 July 56, For Official
Use Only. at

                                        Approved for Release
                                        Date — 1 4 APR 1984

Document 3. File card on Hilda Gadea de Guevara (July 1956)
1956: Similar card on Che Guevara's spouse, Hilda Gadea de Guevara.

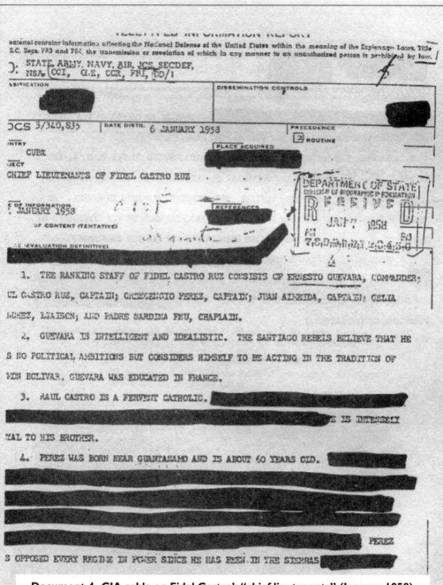

material contains information affecting the National Defense of the United States within the meaning of the Espionage Laws, Title
S.C. Secs. 793 and 794, the transmission or revelation of which in any manner to an unauthorized person is prohibited by law.

): STATE, ARMY, NAVY, AIR, JCS, SECDEF,
): NSA, OCI, O.E, CGR, FPI, DO/1

SSIFICATION   DISSEMINATION CONTROLS

JCS 3/340,835   DATE DISTR. 6 JANUARY 1958   PRECEDENCE
                                                        ☒ ROUTINE
NTRY
   CUBA   PLACE ACQUIRED
JECT
CHIEF LIEUTENANTS OF FIDEL CASTRO RUZ

                                                   DEPARTMENT OF STATE
F OF INFORMATION.   BUREAU OF BIOGRAPHIC INFORMATION
: JANUARY 1958   REFERENCES   R E C E I V E D
UF CONTENT (TENTATIVE)   JAN 7 1958
E (EVALUATION DEFINITIVE)   7:8:9:10:11:12:1:2:3:4:5:6

1. THE RANKING STAFF OF FIDEL CASTRO RUZ CONSISTS OF ERNESTO GUEVARA, COMMANDER;
UL CASTRO RUZ, CAPTAIN; CRESCENCIO PEREZ, CAPTAIN; JUAN ALMEIDA, CAPTAIN; CELIA
GOMEZ, LIAISON; AND PADRE SARDINA FNU, CHAPLAIN.

2. GUEVARA IS INTELLIGENT AND IDEALISTIC. THE SANTIAGO REBELS BELIEVE THAT HE
S NO POLITICAL AMBITIONS BUT CONSIDERS HIMSELF TO BE ACTING IN THE TRADITION OF
MON BOLIVAR. GUEVARA WAS EDUCATED IN FRANCE.

3. RAUL CASTRO IS A FERVENT CATHOLIC. ▓▓▓▓▓▓▓▓▓▓▓▓▓▓▓▓▓▓▓▓
▓▓▓▓▓▓▓▓▓▓▓▓▓▓▓ E IS INTENSELY
YAL TO HIS BROTHER.

4. PEREZ WAS BORN NEAR GUANTANAMO AND IS ABOUT 60 YEARS OLD. ▓▓▓▓▓▓▓▓

▓▓

▓▓

▓▓▓▓▓▓▓▓▓▓▓▓▓▓▓▓▓▓▓▓▓▓▓▓▓▓▓▓▓▓▓▓▓▓▓▓ PEREZ

S OPPOSED EVERY REGIME IN POWER SINCE HE HAS BEEN IN THE SIERRAS ▓▓▓▓▓

Document 4. CIA cable on Fidel Castro's "chief lieutenants" (January 1958)
(a) 1958: Secret CIA cable containing short biographical notes on ranking staff of Fidel
Castro's guerilla force in the Sierra Maestra. Che Guevara is described as "intelligent and
idealistic" and believes himself to be acting in the "tradition of Simon Bolivar." Note the
distribution of cable to Department of State, Army, Navy, Air Force, Joint Chiefs of Staff,
National Security Agency and others.

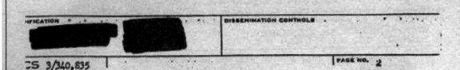

CS 3/340,835   PAGE NO. 2

PEREZ IS IN CHARGE OF THE SECURITY
THE CASTRO HEADQUARTERS AND THE SURROUNDING AREA.

5. SANCHEZ, THE DAUGHTER OF A DOCTOR, STUDIED NURSING IN THE U. S. A. AND IS
RY PRO-U. S.. HER OPINIONS ARE IMPORTANT TO CASTRO.

6. ALMEIDA, THE ONLY NEGRO OFFICER, WAS A TRACTOR MECHANIC IN HAVANA. HE
CEIVED HIS POLITICAL EDUCATION FROM FIDEL CASTRO, WITH WHOM HE WAS IMPRISONED ON
E ISLE OF PINES. HE CAME FROM MEXICO WITH CASTRO AND HAS HIS CONFIDENCE.

7. FIDEL CASTRO IS THE DOMINATING INFLUENCE, AND HIS STAFF IS VERY UNITED.
COMMENT: THE SANTIAGO REBELS BELIEVE BLINDLY IN FIDEL CASTRO BUT ARE APATHETIC
WARDS HIS AIDES. THEY NEITHER KNOW NOR CARE ABOUT THE POLITICAL THOUGHTS AND
PIRATIONS OF THE LATTER.)

LD DISTRIBUTION: NONE

(END OF MESSAGE)

Document 4 (b) 1958.

CENTRAL INTELLIGENCE AGENCY

This material contains information affecting the National Defense of the United States within the meaning of the Espionage Laws, Title 18, U.S.C. Secs. 793 and 794, the transmission or revelation of which in any manner to an unauthorized person is prohibited by law.

COUNTRY Cuba	REPORT NO. CS-3/345,282
SUBJECT The 26 of July Revolutionary Movement Forces—Members of the General Staff	DATE DISTR. 13 February 1958
	NO. PAGES 3
	REQUIREMENT NO.
DATE OF INFO. Mid-January 1958	REFERENCES

SOURCE EVALUATIONS ARE DEFINITIVE. APPRAISAL OF CONTENT IS TENTATIVE.

SOURCE:

1. The general staff of the 26 of July Revolutionary Movement forces, led by Fidel CASTRO Ruz, is currently composed of the following persons:

   a. Ernesto GUEVARA Serna,[1] who has the rank of commander, in charge of rebel forces in the Bueycito area;

3. While he was in Mexico in the summer of 1956 Fidel CASTRO Ruz met Ernesto GUEVARA Serna. GUEVARA, who was at that time employed in a laboratory in Mexico City. GUEVARA was immediately attracted by the prospect of guerrilla warfare, and wanted to help in the fight to correct the existing political situation in Latin America. He said he had done a great deal of travelling, that he had seen great discrepancies, and that he was an idealist. GUEVARA is purported to have joined the CASTRO forces merely because he is inspired by the "romance of fighting", and not so much because of any political ideal.

Document 5. CIA report on general staff of July 26 Movement (January 1958)
1958: CIA report on the general staff of the July 26 Movement. Che Guevara is described as wanting to "help in the fight to correct the existing political situation in Latin America."

SEE BOTTOM OF PAGE FOR SPECIAL CONTROLS IF

INFORMATION REPORT

PARED AND DISSEMINATED BY

CENTRAL INTELLIGENCE AGENCY

This material contains information affecting the National Defense of the United States within the meaning of the Espionage Laws, Title 18, U.S.C. Secs. 793 and 794, the transmission or revelation of which in any manner to an unauthorized person is prohibited by law.

C.C.

Biographic and Personality Information
Concerning "Che" (Ernesto Guevara), Henchman
of Fidel Castro

REPORT NO. 00—B-3,098,099

DATE DISTRIBUTED 13 Feb 58

NO. OF PAGES 4   NO. OF ENCLS.

SUPPLEMENT TO REPORT #

RESPONSIVE TO

00/C-

THIS IS UNEVALUATED INFORMATION

The individual who calls himself "Che" and who is one of Fidel Castro's chief lieutenants is an Argentine medical doctor named Ernesto Guevara. The following represents the information concerning this man. "Che", incidentally, is a familiar form of address. Guevara is never known by any other name.

Document 6. CIA biographical note on Che Guevara (February 1958)

1958: Four-page CIA biographical and personality report concerning Che Guevara, Fidel Castro's "henchman." Apparently this information is gathered from someone in Che's band.

"Che" is between 25 and 30 years old. ▓▓▓▓▓▓▓▓ He is about five feet nine inches tall and weighs about 160 pounds. He is stocky in build, and is strong rather than lean and sinewy. He has brown hair and a brown mustache and beard. His beard, but not the hair on his head, has a very reddish tinge. By no stretch of the imagination, however, can "Che" be described as red-bearded. He has a rather square face, a straight nose, an olive complexion, and dark brown eyes. He is definitely of Spanish descent and does not ▓▓▓▓▓▓▓ have any negro strain in him. In short, he is a "Latino" and not a mulatto. He is, incidentally, extremely proud of his "Latino" background. He bears a rather remarkable resemblance to the Mexican artist Cantinflas and sometimes laughingly refers to himself as "Cantinflas". However, he is never known by the name "Cantinflas". He has rather clownish features. By ordinary middle class standards, "Che" has bad teeth, but by the standards of his companions in the mountains his teeth are perhaps better than the average. "Che" does not wear glasses ▓▓ ▓▓▓▓▓ and has no particularly outstanding mannerisms, with the possible exception of his exuberance and his readiness to laugh. He smiles readily and is extremely personable. "Che" possesses a long scar on the left side of his neck, a scar caused, he says, by a wound received in combat against the Cuban Government forces. ▓▓▓▓▓

▓▓▓▓▓▓ The outstandingly noticeable thing about "Che" from the physical aspect is that he has a severe and chronic case of asthma. His asthma is so severe that he always carries with him a portable asthma inhalator which he uses almost constantly. He is completely dependent for survival upon this inhalator ▓▓▓▓▓▓ and always carries a spare with him in case of emergency. One can always tell when "Che" is in a group, even when he is not to be seen, because of the bellows-like noise which this inhalator makes when in use. ▓▓▓▓▓▓▓ he has had chronic asthma ever since childhood and that he has always had to use the inhalator. The remaining noticeable physical trait of "Che" is his filth. He hates to wash and will never do so. He is filthy, even by the rather low standard of cleanliness prevailing among the Castro forces in the Sierra Maestra. Once in a while "Che" would take some of his men to a stream or pool, in

Document 6 (a) This document emphasizes Che's asthma, claiming that he "is completely dependent for his survival upon his inhalator." Also, includes the statement that Che has no "negro strain in him" and derogatory comments concerning Che's teeth and bathing habits.

order that they might wash. On those occasions "Che" would never wash either himself or his clothes, but would sit on the bank and watch the others. He is really outstandingly and spectacularly dirty.

"Che" speaks fluent Spanish, of course. He speaks French fairly well, although with a heavy Spanish accent. He speaks no English at all, and knows only one word of English. The word is "golf", a game of which he is inordinately fond. ▓▓▓▓▓▓▓ he had learned some Russian in a school in Buenos Aires ▓▓▓▓▓▓▓▓▓▓▓ that on that account he had been called a Communist. ▓▓▓▓▓▓▓ In his opinion the Western world is full of people who call Communists those who show any interest in the USSR. ▓▓▓ ▓now whether or not he can actually speak any Russian▓▓▓▓

"Che" told relatively little concerning his personal background. He claims that his uncle, whom he identified as Guevara-Lynch ▓▓▓▓▓▓▓▓ is or was the Argentine ambassador in Havana, Cuba, and is a naval officer. "Che" was born in Argentina ▓▓▓▓▓ in some city or town other than Buenos Aires. ▓▓▓▓▓▓ His father is a medical doctor in Argentina▓▓▓▓▓▓ the said that his father is still alive. "Che" has some brothers and sisters. ▓▓▓▓▓ He also has a wife and daughter, ▓▓▓▓ Certainly, they are not with him in the Sierra Maestra. ▓▓▓▓ "Che" does come from a middle-class background ▓▓ he is not by origin a "big-city" type.

Document 6 (a) contd.

"Che" asserts that he is a medical doctor and that he is a specialist in allergies. He gave as his reason for being an allergist the sympathy he feels for allergy sufferers. This natural sympathy has been increased ████████ by his own troubles with asthma. In other words, his choice of a medical specialty was dictated by humanitarian, as much as by scientific, motives. ████████████████████████████████ his medical specialization in allergies is a specialization of study rather than a specialization of actual medical practice. At any rate, he is the friend to and sympathizer with the allergy sufferer. ████████

████████ he at least has had some medical training. medical examinations, ████████ had been either an advanced medical student or intern or that of one who had ████████

████ "Che's" present medical activities are much more than those necessary to keep a force of men in being. ████████ among his medical duties is the extraction of teeth and ████████ he much preferred to extract upper teeth. The reason for this taste in tooth extractions ████████ is that he is never quite sure of the location of the nerves in the lower jaw. Consequently he prefers to defer extractions of lower teeth in the hope that the trouble will go away. If it does not, of course, he will undertake the operation.

"Che" smiles and laughs readily, ████████████████ and has an engaging and exuberant personality. He appears ████████ quite a romantic figure in his own mind and to be just the type which would joust at windmills. For instance, although he is a medical doctor and although Castro took him on because a doctor was needed, "Che" delights in referring to himself as a warrior. ████████ "I am not a doctor; I am a warrior".

Document 6 (b)&(c) 1958: The informant alleges that Che Guevara speaks only one word of English — "golf" — a game he supposedly loves and comments on his preference as a doctor to extract upper teeth. Describes Che as "the type which would joust at windmills." "I am not a doctor; I am a warrior," Che is reported to have said.

- 3 -   CO-B-3,098,099

He is extremely proud of being the only one of Castro's officers in the mountains to bear the title of "Comandante". ▓▓▓▓▓▓▓▓ he always had been the rebel in his family. In 1954 he was in Guatemala when Castillo Armas displaced Arbenz. He spoke strongly of this episode and denounced to ▓▓▓▓▓▓ what he claimed was US influence in the successful rebellion by Castillo Armas. He rambled on at considerable length concerning alleged actions against Arbenz by the US. These accounts of his were highly colored and rather extreme and romantic in tone and character. ▓▓▓▓▓▓▓▓ he explained that his reason for feeling as he does concerning the events in Guatemala in 1954 was that he regards the whole thing as an affront to Guatemalan national feeling and national dignity. Concerning the Hungarian revolution of 1956, "Che" sticks straight to the Communist Party line and asserts flatly that the US set off that revolt. He asserts that he left Argentina because of the policies of Perón, but made no claim ▓▓▓▓ that Perón had persecuted or exiled him. He merely chose to leave. His subsequent history is not clear ▓▓▓▓▓▓ he spent some time in Bolivia. Guatemala (see above), and then went to Mexico, where he first met Castro. ▓▓▓▓▓▓▓▓▓▓▓▓▓▓ Apparently, he and Castro liked each other from the start. Castro needed a doctor. "Che" liked the prospect of action in Cuba and accompanied Castro when he went to Cuba in 1956.

Document 6 (d) 1958: Asserts that Che Guevara "always had been the rebel in the family." "Apparently, he and Castro liked each other from the start. Castro needed a doctor. 'Che' liked the idea of action in Cuba ..."

Now, it is of course impossible to state whether or not "Che" is or is not a Communist. He himself denies it. There is no question but that his utterances regarding events in Guatemala and Hungary are definitely Communist in tone and approach. There is no question that he does not entertain friendly feelings towards the US. He repeated with great solemnity and emphasis that the US is planning to cut Cuba physically into two parts by means of a canal. His political views are those of a very emotional "Latino" nationalist. Despite "Che's" undoubted hostility to the US and despite his █████████ of the Communist line concerning Guatemala and Hungary, ███████ difficult to believe that he is a Communist in the sense of the dedicated Party member and revolutionary, and conspirator. One reason██████████ is that he does not talk consistently like an intellectually-disciplined Communist (despite the two examples above). He does not have the usual jargon, the usual phrases, the pat and stock answers which ████ characterize the real Communist. He does not display the patterned thinking which █████ characterizes the real Communist. Furthermore, "Che" is such an individualist and such a romantic that he doesn't sound like an "organization man" at all. Of course, this may be nothing but camouflage, ██████████████████. "Che's" attitude towards the US ████████ is an attitude which is fairly common among young "Latinos". He has the emotional hostility of the nationalist inhabitant of a small and backward and weak country towards the big and rich and strong country. It does not seem ██████████ the organized, directed hostility which characterizes Communist hostility. Curiously enough, in "Che's" case this unfriendly attitude towards the US is coupled with a desire to visit the US and admire its wonders (his phrase). In sum, ██████████ "Che's" attitude towards the US is dictated more by somewhat childish emotionalism and jealousy and resentment than by a cold, reasoned, intellectual decision. Of course, the effect may well be the same. It is the origin which is different.████

"Che" is fairly intellectual for a "Latino". He is quite well-read in "Latino" literature and has an appreciation of the classics from other literatures. He is intelligent and quick.██████████████████████ he has caused books to be brought into the Sierra Maestra and by the way he reads to the soldiers

- 4 -   00-B-3,098,099

in his column ██████ never saw him reading Karl Marx or other Communist authors. On the contrary, he confines to literature his efforts to educate his soldiers ██████████████████ reading to them from the works of Charles Dickens and of Alphonse Daudet, among others.

██████████████ "Che" has a conception of himself as a romantic, dashing, warrior figure. He claims that he has no political influence over Castro and that he does not want to have any. Politics, as such, does not interest him. ██████ that if Castro wins his fight, he ("Che") will leave Cuba and explore the upper reaches of the Amazon River. However, "Che" now considers himself a Cuban and as of the present moment intends to become a Cuban citizen after Castro wins his rebellion (which "Che" is sure he will). This is something he has always wanted to do, ██████ said he. He is an adventurer, not a politician or a professional revolutionar ██████████ "Che" has always been searching for something with which to give his life some meaning and significance and that for the time being he has found it in Castro, not Castro the politician, but in Castro the underdog, in Castro the fighter against tyranny.

He is an individualist. "Che" stated more than once ██████ that if Castro's rebellion does not succeed, he, "Che", will "die like a man" at the head of his troops. ██████ he would probably make the effort to do just that, because he is a combat man, because he would feel it incumbent upon himself to set the example to his troops of courage in the face of heavy odds. "Che" is not, ██████ the leader to direct things from behind. He must be out in front, inspiring his troops by his own deeds of valor. If this sounds romantic, ██████ "Che" is, a romantic.

██████████████ "Che's" attitude concerning the burning of the sugar crop and concerning bombing and terrorism, but think that he would either consider these matters as beneath his dignity to consider or else would consider them childish, just as the mountain forces of Castro consider all other manifestations of the rebellion against Batista as childish.

- END -

Document 6 (f) 1958: Che Guevara "has a concept of himself as a romantic, dashing, warrior figure." "Politics, as such, does not interest him," and "if Castro wins his fight, he ('Che') will leave Cuba and explore the upper reaches of the Amazon River." Reports that Che reads literature to his troops, including Charles Dickens and Alphonse Daudet, and describes himself as an "individualist." Indicates that if Fidel does not succeed, he "will 'die like a man' at the head of his troops."

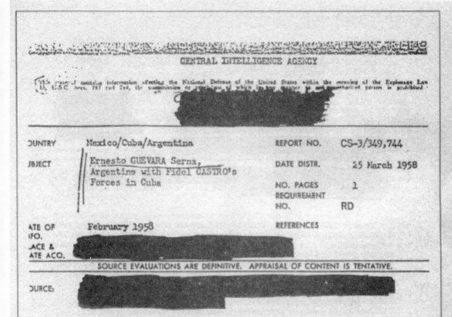

CENTRAL INTELLIGENCE AGENCY

This material contains information affecting the National Defense of the United States within the meaning of the Espionage Laws, U.S.C. Secs. 793 and 794, the transmission or revelation of which in any manner to an unauthorized person is prohibited.

COUNTRY	Mexico/Cuba/Argentina	REPORT NO.	CS-3/349,744
SUBJECT	Ernesto GUEVARA Serna, Argentine with Fidel CASTRO's Forces in Cuba	DATE DISTR.	25 March 1958
		NO. PAGES	1
		REQUIREMENT NO.	RD
DATE OF INFO.	February 1958	REFERENCES	
PLACE & DATE ACQ.			

SOURCE EVALUATIONS ARE DEFINITIVE. APPRAISAL OF CONTENT IS TENTATIVE.

SOURCE:

Dr. Ernesto GUEVARA Serna, an Argentine with Fidel CASTRO Ruz' forces in Cuba, is not a Communist Party member. Although he does not have deep Communist convictions, he is a Communist-sympathizer.

Headquarters Comment.

. According to a source GUEVARA joined the CASTRO forces in the Sierra Maestra Mountains in February 1957.

Document 7. CIA report on Che Guevara's communist sympathies (February 1958)
CIA report noting that Che Guevara is not a Communist Party member although "he is a Communist-sympathizer."

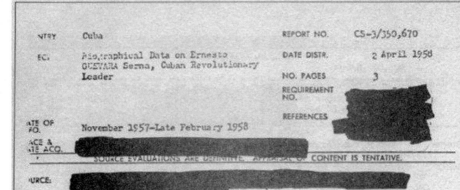

1. Ernesto GUEVARA Serna, commander of one of Fidel CASTRO's detachments in the Sierra Maestra Mountains, an Argentine national, is about 29 years of age, is married, and has a two-year-old daughter. His wife and child are presumed to be living in Buenos Aires at the present time. Although GUEVARA pursued medical studies, he is not interested in physical healing in general; he is sympathetic only to victims of asthma, because he himself has suffered from persistent and chronic asthma since infancy. Frequently during marches with the CASTRO forces, GUEVARA suffers asthmatic attacks and has to treat himself with medicines and an inhaler which he always carries with him.

2. GUEVARA belongs to a middle-class family. He has pleasing manners, speaks French fluently, and has a good cultural background. He is familiar with such writers as Malaparte[1] and Koestler.[2] His life-long ambition has been to become a revolutionary fighter. He has never been to the United States, although he has traveled extensively in Central America and South America. On occasion he has described his experiences on the Bolivian plateau and in Mexico. From his references to Guatemala it is apparent that GUEVARA was in that country at the time Carlos CASTILLO Armas overthrew the regime of Jacobo Arbenz and assumed power. GUEVARA was apparently on the side of the Arbenz forces, since he criticizes the United States bitterly for helping to oust Arbenz. GUEVARA claims that the late John Peurifoy, then United States Ambassador to Guatemala, told Arbenz he could remain in power if he rounded up and killed his Communist followers. According to GUEVARA, when Arbenz refused to do this the United States sent warplanes into Guatemala to help overthrow him, and Arbenz' own chief of staff was bribed to turn against him. GUEVARA claims that CASTILLO Armas was then able to seize control of the country with American weapons. When CASTILLO Armas came into power GUEVARA's wife was taken to the border by Guatemalan police; she was given the equivalent of five dollars in United States currency and expelled from the country.

Document 8. CIA biographical data on Che Guevara (November 1957 – February 1958)

1958: Three-page CIA biographical report on Che Guevara.

(a) Discusses Che's "chronic" asthma, his literary interests, his desire "to become a revolutionary fighter" and his support for Arbenz in Guatemala.

One of GUEVARA's principal and most emotional preoccupations is the subject of what he considers United States interference in Latin American affairs and the resultant anti-democratic proceedings against nationalist or leftist public figures, i.e. SANDINO in Nicaragua, Jose MENENDEZ (sic), and others. GUEVARA is keenly aware of Latin America's inferior position in the world. He feels that the Latin Americans have made no contribution to the world. He resents bitterly the resultant handicaps of Latins trying to compete with advanced Westerners, and he resents the fact that at any job the American always has to be the boss. He feels that in social and political matters the role of Latin America has been one of neglect. As an example of this, he remarked on one occasion, "Five thousand workers are shot down on the Bolivian highlands, and maybe there is one line in the New York papers, which mentions that there is labor unrest in Bolivia." He wonders if the United States so-called international labor unions would take an interest in the South American worker and if it might help to raise the living standards of the Latin Americans to a level which might come closer to that of the North Americans.

4. GUEVARA's thinking does not appear to follow any fixed economic or sociological pattern. He has denied vehemently that he is, or that he ever was, a Communist. In fact, his thinking seems to be far removed from the orthodox Marxist pattern. GUEVARA would be described more accurately as a Latino populist, with a touch of the intellectual's self-focused searching and an intense degree of ultra-nationalistic Latin pride. GUEVARA, like Malraux's 3revolutionaries, seeks a meaning for his own life before anything else.

5. In his present role as commander of Fidel CASTRO's No. 2. column, GUEVARA seems to have found deep fulfillment. He does not appear to be troubled with such frequent asthma. Except for a scar on his neck directly under his jaw, the result of a nearly-fatal bullet wound sustained in fighting at Alegria in December 1956, he is unscathed and in high spirits.4 He watches over his troops with paternal concern, and his men worship him. In the evening they gather around him like children, and he reads adventure stories to them. The rebel soldiers call him muy valiente (very brave fellow), which is about the highest term of approbation in the Sierra Maestra Mountains. His popularity is second only to that of Fidel CASTRO. He appears to be much more popular than Raul CASTRO, who is somewhat a martinet, is harsh, impatient, and self-righteous.

6. GUEVARA disclaims all political ambitions beyond helping CASTRO to achieve victory. He plans to settle in Cuba when the fighting is over; however, he does not seem to be the type of person to settle permanently in one place. GUEVARA sometimes talks about organizing an expedition in the future to explore the upper reaches of the Amazon and the Orinoco Valleys.5

Headquarters Comments

1. Presumed to be a reference to Curzio Malaparte, Italian leftist writer who died recently. Malaparte, one of the founding members of the Italian Fascist Party in 1919, wrote, among other books, The Skin and Caputt. Malaparte claimed to be strongly opposed to any form of totalitarianism.

Document 8 (b) 1958: Describes Che Guevara's views of U.S. interference in Latin American affairs. Che's thinking is considered "far removed from the orthodox Marxist patter"; he is described as more of a "Latino" populist. He is the commander of Fidel Castro's second guerilla column and his men "worship him."

2. Presumed to be a reference to Arthur Koestler, who was born in Budapest in 1905 and joined the Communist Party of Hungary in 1931. Koestler left the Party at the time of the Moscow trials in 1938. He has lived in the United States, England, and France. He is the author of many novels, among them, Darkness at Noon, Spanish Testament, Scum of the Earth, Arrow in the Blue, and Invisible Writing. The two latter books are an autobiography of the author: Arrow in the Blue describes Koestler's life to his 27th year, and Invisible Writing is a detailed account of his seven years in the Communist Party of Hungary.

3. Presumed to be a reference to Andre Malraux, a Frenchman by birth, who went to Indo-China at an early age. He became involved in politics there and also wrote several books based on life in Indo-China. He was acting as associate secretary-general of the Kuomintang in China in 1925, at a time when the Kuomintang had a number of members who admired the Soviet Union. Malraux played a leading role in the National Liberation Movement of China. One of his books, Man's Fate, dramatizes the Chinese Revolution of 1924, in which he participated. Another one of his books, Days of Wrath, depicts the heroism of Communists under the regime of Adolph Hitler in Germany.

Comments

4. During late November or early December 1957 GUEVARA was wounded in the leg. This wound was serious enough to warrant his evacuation from the Sierra Maestra Mountains to Manzanillo.

5. In January 1958 said that GUEVARA was no longer an Argentine citizen. He claimed that a ceremony conferring Cuban citizenship on GUEVARA had been performed by Fidel CASTRO Ruz in the Sierra Maestra Mountains. Although this act has no validity, it is possibly intended to provide an acceptable basis for the formal granting of citizenship when and if the revolution is successful.

Document 8 (c) 1958: Mentions a wound Che Guevara had, and that Fidel had conferred citizenship on him.

CENTRAL INTELLIGENCE AGENCY

TELETYPED INFORMATION REPORT

███████ ████ ██████████ effecting the National Defense of the United States within the meaning of the Espionage Laws, Title U.S.C., Secs 793 and 794, the possession or revelation of which in any manner to an unauthorized person is prohibited by law

TO: STATE, ARMY, NAVY, AIR, JCS, SECDEF, FBI,
NSA, CIA, OCI

CLASSIFICATION   DISSEMINATION CONTROLS

                                                                         B1

TDCS 3/350,959 | DATE DISTR. 3 April 1958 | PRECEDENCE
                                              ☑ ROUTINE

COUNTRY
Cuba   PLACE ACQUIRED   DEPARTMENT OF STATE
SUBJECT   ███████████
Ernesto GUEVARA Serna, Lieutenant of Fidel CASTRO Ruz   *RECEIVED*
                                                                   APR 7 1958
DATE OF INFORMATION   REFERENCES   *1 2 3 4 5*
2 April 1958
APPRAISAL OF CONTENT (TENTATIVE)   A

SOURCE (EVALUATION DEFINITIVE)

Ernesto GUEVARA Serna, Commander of Column No. 4 of the CASTRO forces, claims that the campaign of the Sierra Maestra is based on Regional Clandestine Committee Acts (sic), a Soviet post-war publication which has been translated and is published in Mexico. GUEVARA is anti-American. He is not a Marxist, but he follows blindly the Communist Party line in all issues. Although he may not be a registered Communist Party member, he is an easy target for the Communists.

████████. GUEVARA has a police record in Miami, Florida, where he was arrested and interrogated during the Korean War. He was once employed by a news agency sponsored by Juan PERON, former Argentine President. Gilda GADES, his wife, formerly worked in Mexico for the United Nations as an economist).

Field Distribution   None

End of Message

Document 9. CIA information report that Guevara commands guerilla column (April 1958)
    1958: CIA report stating that Che Guevara commands Column No. 4 of the Castro forces, that he is "anti-American," and that he has a police record in Miami where he was arrested and interrogated during the Korean War. (If this is so, it must have been during his 1952 visit.)

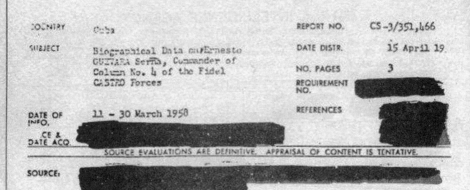

COUNTRY	Cuba	REPORT NO.	CS-3/351,466
SUBJECT	Biographical Data on Ernesto GUEVARA Serna, Commander of Column No. 4 of the Fidel CASTRO Forces	DATE DISTR.	15 April 19.
		NO. PAGES	3
		REQUIREMENT NO.	
DATE OF INFO.	11 - 30 March 1958	REFERENCES	
CE & DATE ACQ.			

SOURCE EVALUATIONS ARE DEFINITIVE.   APPRAISAL OF CONTENT IS TENTATIVE.

SOURCE:

1. Ernesto GUEVARA Serna ("Che") was born in Rosario, Province of Santa Fe, Argentina, on 6 June 1928. His parents still live in Rosario. He is Commander of Column No. 4 of the 26 of July Revolutionary Movement forces in the Sierra Maestra, the largest of the five columns under the command of Fidel CASTRO Ruz. GUEVARA studied medicine at the University of Buenos Aires. While at the University of Buenos Aires he expressed his opposition to Juan PERON, then dictator of Argentina, and later voted against him. In 1953, when GUEVARA was called for his compulsory military service, he refused to serve under PERON and for that reason left Argentina. He visited Bolivia, Peru, Ecuador, Panama, Costa Rica, Nicaragua, Honduras, Guatemala, Mexico, and Cuba.

2. GUEVARA specialized in allergies and for that reason has done a great deal of physiological research. When he graduated from medical school he did some work in this field with a doctor in Buenos Aires. Later in Mexico he apparently tried to resume this research. He never established a medical practice. In Mexico he married a Peruvian exile who was an Aprista and they have a two-year-old daughter. It is rumored that GUEVARA and his wife are separated. He has mentioned on occasion that she may have returned to Peru since the change of administration in that country.

3. GUEVARA was in Guatemala during the last days of the regime of Jacobo Arbenz and defended the latter in the Guatemalan press. After the fall of Arbenz GUEVARA went to Mexico where he joined the 26 of July Revolutionary Movement of Fidel CASTRO Ruz. While in Mexico he received training in mountain warfare. GUEVARA was to serve the CASTRO Movement in the capacity of contact surgeon. He is one of the twelve survivors of the GRAMA expedition led by CASTRO which landed in Cuba on 2 December 1956. During the sixteen months in the Sierra Maestra with the forces of Fidel CASTRO, GUEVARA abandoned his post as combat surgeon to assume command of one of CASTRO's columns.

Document 10. CIA biographical data on Che Guevara (March 11-30, 1958)
Three pages of CIA biographical data on Che Guevara.
(a) Che voted against Perón, refused to serve in the Argentine military and left Argentina for that reason. Che was one of the 12 survivors of the *Granma* expedition.

GUEVARA claims emphatically that he is not now, nor has he ever been a Communist. He is a self-acclaimed individualist, a non-conformist, and an ultranationalist in the Latin American sense. He resents accusations that he is a Communist and blames the United States and the United Press for such charges. GUEVARA claims that he defended the regime of Arbenz in Guatemala because he believed in the rise of an American republic which could defend itself against exploitation by foreign capital, for example, by the United Fruit Company. He refuses to believe that there was a Soviet penetration in Guatemala during the regime of Arbenz, and he said that all Latin Americans resented United States interference in the affairs of Guatemala.

GUEVARA said he became interested in Cuba during his university days when he read several books on Jose MARTI, the Cuban patriot. Later he met several Cuban exiles in Guatemala who were members of the 26 of July Revolutionary Movement. The aims and the ideals of the Movement appealed to GUEVARA, so he joined the organization.

GUEVARA is well-mannered, soft-spoken, and hesitant in conversation. He is extremely popular throughout the 26 of July Movement, both among the civilian and military components of the organization. In spite of his gentle nature he seems to have better military command than most of the leaders of the Movement. He is energetic, athletic, participates in any type of activity about the camp no matter whether it is softball, general recreation, or caring for pets. His men respect him because he is daring in combat and never passes up an opportunity for an encounter. He is the only commander in the Movement who has ever been observed to stand a man at attention and discipline him for inefficiency.

GUEVARA is about 5'11" tall, weighs about 170 lbs, and has a medium build. He is very tanned, but normally his complexion is very fair. He has crudely cut, dark brown hair, brown eyes, a rather high forehead, and a sparse brown beard. He generally wears olive-drab combat dungarees and a black turtle-neck wool sweater. His dungaree and vest pockets are used as files for messages, and are always stuffed with papers.

GUEVARA suffers from chronic asthma and must use his inhaler at night and during marches. Fidel CASTRO has ordered him to ride whenever possible during marches.

GUEVARA's sense of humor seemed to overcome his vexation when asked about Communism during a recent United Press interview. He answered that he was not a Communist, but that such questions from the press and indirectly from the United States Government were inducive to becoming a Communist. Later, when asked why he had abandoned his country, his profession, his wife and child for a distant ideological cause, he answered with mirth that this could have been a result of two factors: 1) that he read MARTI as a boy, or 2) because of the rubles he had hidden in his headquarters. In the same interview he was questioned concerning the duration and hardship of the struggle in the mountains and how long morale of the Movement would hold up. He answered that they have all the time in the world; that they are constantly growing; that only 12 men survived the landing 15 months previously but that there were now 1,200 men in the Sierra Maestra fighting forces.

Document 10 (b) 1958: Guevara says he defended Arbenz so that Guatemala could defend itself against "exploitation by foreign capital," particularly the United Fruit Company. He became interested in Cuba during his university days when he read books by José Marti.

CS-3/352,466

- 3 -

GUEVARA spends most of this time on combat missions. During his absence
from his headquarters Ramiro VALDES, his second-in-command, takes over. When
GUEVARA is in camp his typical day begins at 7 a.m. He has early coffee,
plays with a dog or cat, and then wanders out for his morning tea.
Messages and visitors begin to arrive about 8:30 a.m. Headquarters business
may range from cases of military discipline to logistics, or to arbitration
in cases of military transaction involving the property of farmers. Since
his command is a base installation, the paper work is relatively heavy
for a guerrilla movement. In the afternoon he may be needed at a civilian
or military trial. Offenses involved may range from something as light as
property liability to something as serious as treason. By evening he is
ready to listen to news broadcasts or chat with camp visitors. He retires
at 9 p.m., when he lights his carbide lamp, and a huge cigar, and
brings out his book on Jose MARTI.

Headquarters' Comment.   CS-3/350,670
                              contain additional information on Ernesto
GUEVARA Serna.

Document 10 (c) 1958: Describes a typical day in Che Guevara's life as a guerilla. He spends "most of his time on combat missions," and at night smokes a "huge cigar" and reads José Marti.

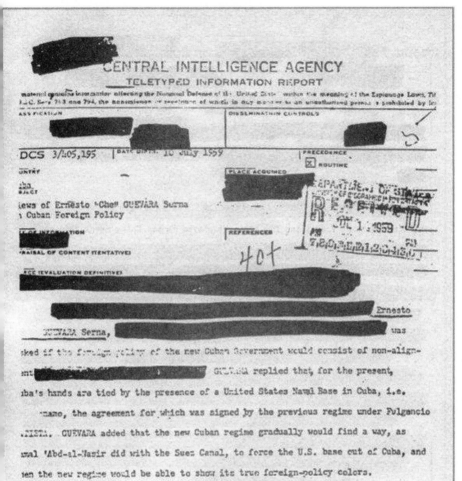

Document 11. CIA information report on Guevara's views on foreign policy (July 1959)
1959: CIA information report on "Views of Ernesto 'Che' Guevara Serna on Cuban Foreign Policy."

_UNTRY	Cuba/Latin America	REPORT NO.	CS -3/406,916
_JECT	Views of Ernesto "Che" GUEVARA, Cuban Revolutionary Leader	DATE DISTR.	28 July 1959
		NO. PAGES	2
		REFERENCES	RD

TE OF
_?
ACE &
TE ACQ.   FIELD REPORT NO.

SOURCE EVALUATIONS ARE DEFINITIVE. APPRAISAL OF CONTENT IS TENTATIVE.

RCE:

1. The policy of the United States in Latin America is wrong and will have to change, in the interest of the U.S. Whatever the intentions of the American people may be, the U.S. Government and U. S. business firms have, in fact, supported dictators from one end of Latin America to the other, notably BATISTA, TRUJILLO, and PEREZ Jimenez. In Cuba the revolutionary movement was opposed by BATISTA forces using U. S. planes, which dropped U. S. napalm. The CASTRO government has letters and documentary proof showing improper collaboration between the former U. S. Ambassador and the BATISTA regime. The U. S. military mission gave tactical advice to the BATISTA forces in their attempted suppression of the revolution. The U. S. sent spies into the CASTRO camp in the guise of journalists or others, whose information was then relayed to the BATISTA regime.

2. GUEVARA still remains suspicious of U. S. intentions toward Cuba. He said that there has been a build-up at Guantanamo Bay since the CASTRO victory which is not justified by any local unrest. The precedent of U. S. intervention in Guatemala is not forgotten. CASTRO's remark that, "if the Marines landed, there would be 200,000 dead gringos" was not intended for public consumption and was most unfortunate. However, it did contain a moral: everyone acknowledged the overwhelming power of the U. S., but the Cuban revolutionaries were willing to die to the last man if need be.

3. GUEVARA feels he is unfairly treated by the U. S. press. Reports that there were two Russian advisors with CASTRO, that Marxist indoctrination centers had been established, and that GUEVARA is himself a Communist are untrue. The U. S. press is prone to brand people as Communists who are fighting for freedom from tyranny, from economic domination by foreign companies, and from interference by such companies in local politics, which are legitimate aims. Rightly or wrongly, the U. S. is viewed throughout Latin America as the enemy of popular and reform movements.

4. The U. S. made a great mistake in Guatemala. Although Arbenz and some others were Communists, the movement in Guatemala was essentially a popular one, the people versus United Fruit Company. GUEVARA feels more strongly about this than about U. S. aid to BATISTA. His then wife was dragged through the streets by the forces of CASTILLO Arras. Guatemala

Document 11 contd.

- 2 -

w.. in ...e ...c victory, perhaps, for United Fruit, but it alienated a whole generation of Latin Americans.

5. The coming year will see popular upheavals throughout Latin America— Nicaragua, the Dominican Republic, Colombia, Paraguay. In Argentina Frondizi has no power of his own but retains power by acting as a balance-wheel between the Army and the people. The editor of La Prensa had said that Frondizi had achieved the miracle of alienating both the Communists and the free press at the same time. Brazil had much poverty and distress but had achieved a certain political stability.

6. With respect to the future of U. S. business in Cuba, the U. S. note accepting the principles of agrarian reform and the right of nationalization was gratifying. The difficulty would lie in the valuation of properties. It was not Cuba's intention to drive out U. S. business or force it to the wall, but Cuba did insist on controlling foreign business within its borders to prevent injustices of the past and interference in local politics.

7. Whatever the respective motives might be, the fact is that U. S. influence or equipment was being used to suppress popular movement in Latin America, whereas the Communist bloc was supporting such popular movements around the world. In Cuba the Communists at first had hoped to take over the revolutionary movement, but, when they realized that the people were behind CASTRO, they fell into line, which was a prudent thing for them to do.

8. The United States has achieved social justice and liberty for its own people, but it objects when small Latin American countries struggle for the same things for themselves. This policy is inconsistent and doomed to failure.

Department ... Co

Document 11 contd.

GUEVARA, Ernesto "Che"   CUBA
   March 1960

Che Guevara is the most intellectual member of the group. He
creates fear because of his reserve, giving the impression of
holding back more than he is saying. While he does not cause the
antagonism that Raul does, the fact that he is a foreigner is a
major factor preventing his ever being the leader. He knows
that he cannot force matters to a showdown. He tried to avoid
the foreign visits but had to give in to Fidel. He is not really
the "gray eminence"behind Castro, who gets out to the people too
much and is too individualistic to be so controlled. Of course,
Che does present his point of view well and strongly, but his
position is not so important as reported in the US press. This is
more of a legend because of his inaccessibility than the true
picture. He is certainly a Marxist, a great admirer of the USSR,
but a party-liner would hardly praise such a deviationist as Tito.
I am not actually sure that he is a communist party member and do
not think that he is directed by Moscow.

CIA 00-B-3,155,060, 6 April 1960, CUBA,

**Document 12. CIA report that Guevara is a Marxist but not a "party-liner"
(March 1960)**
    CIA document that is most likely from an informant inside Cuba. States he is a
Marxist, but probably not a "party-liner," as evidenced by his praise of President Tito of
Yugoslavia.

December 3, 1962

Three indicators from Cuba that worry me are:

1.   This

would suggest that we soon would face the prospect of operational SAM

sites manned by Soviets.

2. Che Guevara's statement to the London Daily Worker that

peace has been assurred and that Cuba will pursue the arms struggle

already xx taking place in a number of Latin American countries such as

Venezuela, Guatemalam Paraguzy and Colombia. This would indicate no intentio

to halt Castro sub version in Latin America.

3. Mikoyan's public statement in Moscow that he had achieved Soviet

objective of maintaining a Communist regime in the Western hemisphere.

These three statements would prompt extreme caution on the part

of the United States in any agreement which might give Castro and the

Communists a sanctuary.

John A. McCone
Director

Document 13. CIA memo on Guevara's *Daily Worker* interview from director John McCone (December 3, 1962)

1962: Document from John A. McCone, Director of the CIA, possibly to the Secretary of State or the President concerning an agreement with the Soviet Union regarding Cuba. Specifically mentions as one of three negative "indicators" Che Guevara's *Daily Worker* interview on armed struggle. McCone says "Cuba will pursue the arms [sic] struggle already taking place in a number of Latin American countries ..."

OUTGOING TELEGRAM Department of State   *Brunley 28*

INDICATE: ☐ COLLECT
☐ CHARGE TO   ~~CONFIDENTIAL~~

ACTION: USUN NEW YORK   PRIORITY   1531 **ADVANCE COPY**

          FOR STEVENSON AND McCLOY

          With reference to current negotiations with Kuznetzov, White

House wants to be positive that you are aware of following excerpt
                                                           Che
from XXX Guevara interview with Havana correspondent of London

Daily Worker contained in FBIS No. 70, November 29:

QUOTE
          My final question to Major Guevara was on the contribution

that the Cuban revolution has made to the development of Marxist

thought and practice. His reply was typically modest, and he

deliberately limited himself to the effects of the Cuban example

in Latin America. "The Cuban revolution," he said, "has shown

that in conditions of imperialist domination such as exist in

Latin America, there is no solution but armed struggle--for the

people to take power out of the hands of the Yankee imperialists

and the small group of the national bourgeoisie who work with

them.' The question then was, he added, how this armed struggle

could be most effectively carried through. While the bourgeoisie

had their armed forces concentrated in the cities where they had

---

Drafted by:
S/S-Mr. Little:amp   12/7/62 | Telegraphic transmission and classification approved by: | S-ESLittle

Clearances:
          IO-Mr. Handyside
          White House - Bromley Smith

                                                          REPRODUCTION FROM THIS
                          DECLASSIFIED   COPY IS PROHIBITED
                                                          UNLESS "UNCLASSIFIED".
FORM
8-61 DS-322   E.O. 11652, Sec. 3(3) and 5(D) or (E)
                       By _____ RANS, Date 3/29/74   ~~CONFIDENTIAL~~

**Document 14. Department of State telegram on negotiations with the
USSR (December 7, 1962)**
    1962: Telegram from State Department to the U.S. Ambassador to the United
Nations, Adlai Stevenson, regarding negotiations with the Soviet Union. Once again,
it warns them about Che Guevara's comments on armed struggle in the *Daily Worker*
interview, and quotes the pertinent sections.

the factory workers at their mercy. They were comparatively weak
in the countryside, where the peasants are living mostly in a state
of feudal oppression and are also very revolutionary.

"Cuba has shown," he continued, "that small guerrilla groups,
well-led and located in key points, with strong links with the masses
of the people, can act as a catalyst of the masses bringing them into
mass struggle through action. "Such action, to be convincing, must
be effective, and guerrilla action has shown how armed forces can
be beaten and how guerrillas can be converted into an army which
eventually can destroy the armed forces of the class enemy.
                                    continued
"We say," Major Guevara continued, "that this can be done in a
large number of Latin American countries. But this is not to say
that Cuba's example is to be followed mechanically, but rather
adapted to the specific conditions in each of Latin America's 20
rußa countries." He pointed out that in Venezuela, Guatemala,
Paraguay, and Colombia, guerrillas are already active in armed struggle
against the American imperialists and their henchmen, while there have
been clashes in Nicaragua and Peru, and none of this had any physical
connection with Cuba.

"There is no other solution possible in these countries except
armed struggle. The objective conditions for this exist, and Cuba's
example has shown these countries the way."
                                    UNQUOTE

                                    END

Document 14 contd.

Headquarters
14 JAN 1964

MEMORANDUM FOR :   Special Agent in Charge

SUBJECT   :   GUEVARA de la Serna, Ernesto
                     aka Che
                     #261 746   F   SD/4

1.

2.   As Office of Origin, you are requested to obtain a copy of Subject's fingerprints subsequent to August 1952.

3.   Attached is the biographic information available on Subject.

4.   A deadline of 28 January 1964 has been established in this case.

Attachment
    Control Cards
    Bio Data

Approved for Release
Date 2 6 ...

jh
14 Jan 64
PENDING

E 82

Document 15. FBI request for more recent copies of Che's fingerprints (January 14, 1964)

1964: Request from FBI headquarters for a more recent copy of Che Guevara's fingerprints. What is the reason for the request at this particular time? Did they suspect Che of a crime? Of traveling as a guerilla fighter? Of using a disguise? Did they have a plot to kill him and wanted to make sure they got the right guy?

CENTRAL INTELLIGENCE AGENCY '
● ROUTINE

Intelligence Information ● Cable

IY CUBA   TDCS DB-315/03208-65

28 SEPTEMBER 1965   DISTR. 1 OCTOBER 1965

———— SUBJECT ————

CASTRO'S STATEMENT ON "FREEDOM OF EXODUS" FROM CUBA

Q.   REF   IN -63258

                                           FILE REPORT NO.

1. HEADQUARTERS COMMENT: IN A 28 SEPTEMBER SPEECH AT CERE-
MONIES AT THE PLAZA DE LA REVOLUCION IN HAVANA MARKING THE FIFTH
ANNIVERSARY OF THE FOUNDING OF THE COMMITTEE FOR THE DEFENSE OF THE
REVOLUTION, CUBAN PREMIER FIDEL CASTRO RUZ INDICATED THAT A PUBLIC
CEREMONY WOULD BE HELD IN THE NEXT FEW DAYS IN WHICH THE NEW CENTRAL
COMMITTEE OF THE PARTIDO UNIDO DE LA REVOLUCION SOCIALISTA (PURS,
UNITED PARTY OF THE SOCIALIST REVOLUTION) WOULD BE ANNOUNCED. CASTRO
PROMISED THAT AT THIS CEREMONY A DOCUMENT WOULD BE READ WHICH EX-
PLAINED THE ABSENCE, SINCE MID-MARCH 1965, OF MINISTER OF INDUSTRIES
ERNESTO "CHE" GUEVARA SERNA. IN THIS SAME SPEECH CASTRO INVITED
PERSONS DISAFFECTED WITH HIS REGIME TO LEAVE CUBA, AND HE CITED

CIA ARMY/ACSI NAVY AIR JCS SECDEF NSA NIC OCI OCR
REPCINCLANT CIA/NMCC

**Document 16. CIA report on Fidel's statement about Guevara's "absence"
(September 28, 1965)**
1965: CIA report noting that Fidel Castro says he will read a statement at a
forthcoming public ceremony which will explain Che Guevara's absence.

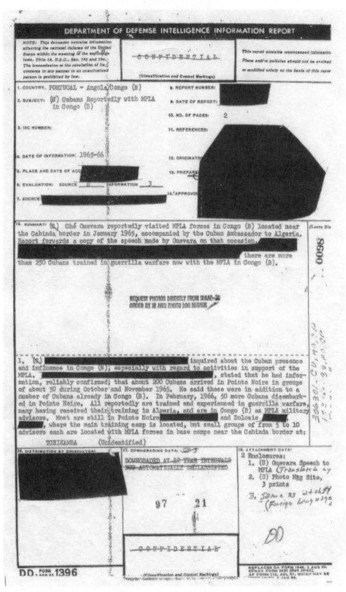

Document 17. Dept. of Defense Intelligence Information Report on Che's visit to MPLA (Popular Movement for the Liberation of Angola) guerilla fighters in the Congo (1965–1966)

Che along with the Cuban ambassador to Algeria visits the MPLA (Popular Movement for the Liberation of Angola) guerilla fighters in the Congo. The document reports that some 250 Cubans are fighting on behalf of the MPLA. Che gives a speech to the MPLA fighters which was translated from the Portuguese by the U.S. and distributed to the intelligence community.

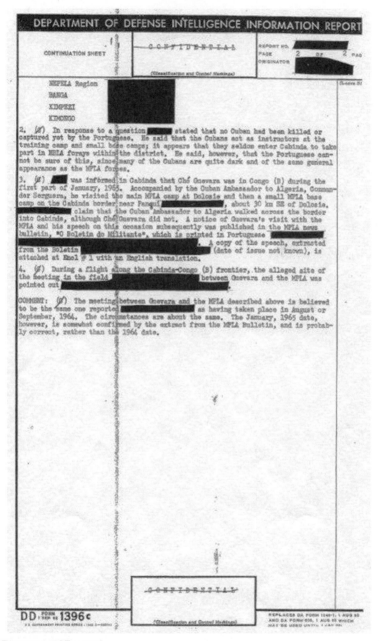

DEPARTMENT OF DEFENSE INTELLIGENCE INFORMATION REPORT

CONTINUATION SHEET	C O N F I D E N T I A L	REPORT NO. ▮▮▮▮
		PAGE 2 OF 2 PAG
	(Classification and Control Markings)	ORIGINATOR ▮▮▮▮

NEPELA Region

BANGA

KIMPEZI

KIMONGO

2. (C) In response to a question ▮▮▮▮ stated that no Cuban had been killed or captured yet by the Portuguese. He said that the Cubans act as instructors at the training camp and small base camps; it appears that they seldom enter Cabinda to take part in NELA forays within the district. He said, however, that the Portuguese cannot be sure of this, since many of the Cubans are quite dark and of the same general appearance as the MPLA forces.

3. (C) ▮▮▮▮ was informed in Cabinda that Ché Guevara was in Congo (B) during the first part of January, 1965. Accompanied by the Cuban Ambassador to Algeria, Commander Sergueza, he visited the main MPLA camp at Dolosie and then a small MPLA base camp on the Cabinda border near Panqui ▮▮▮▮, about 30 km SE of Dolosie. ▮▮▮▮ claim that the Cuban Ambassador to Algeria walked across the border into Cabinda, although Ché Guevara did not. A notice of Guevara's visit with the MPLA and his speech on this occasion subsequently was published in the MPLA news bulletin, "O Boletin do Militante", which is printed in Portuguese ▮▮▮▮ from the Boletin ▮▮▮▮ (date of issue not known), is attached at Encl # 1 with an English translation.

4. (C) During a flight along the Cabinda-Congo (B) frontier, the alleged site of the meeting in the field ▮▮▮▮ between Guevara and the MPLA was pointed out ▮▮▮▮.

COMMENT: (C) The meeting between Guevara and the MPLA described above is believed to be the same one reported ▮▮▮▮ as having taken place in August or September, 1964. The circumstances are about the same. The January, 1965 date, however, is somewhat confirmed by the extract from the MPLA Bulletin, and is probably correct, rather than the 1964 date.

C O N F I D E N T I A L

(Classification and Control Markings)

DD FORM 1396c

REPLACES DA FORM 1048-1, 1 AUG 60 AND DA FORM 600, 1 AUG 60 WHICH MAY BE USED UNTIL 1 JAN 66.

Document 17 contd.

CENTRAL INTELLIGENCE AGENCY

This material contains information affecting the National Defense of the United States within the meaning of the Espionage Laws, T. 18, U.S.C. Secs. 793 and 794, the transmission or revelation of which in any manner to an unauthorized person is prohibited by l

COUNTRY Cuba/Bolivia	REPORT NO. OO-K-323/06978-6
SUBJECT Revolutionary Group Allegedly Bound For Bolivia	DATE DISTR. 23 Apr 66
	NO. PAGES 1
	REFERENCES

DATE OF
O.
CE &
E ACO

THIS IS UNEVALUATED INFORMATION

SOURCE

In the very near future 90 Cuban-trained revolutionaries will depart for Bolivia. They have undergone extensive training in guerrilla warfare and regional Bolivian cultural customs. The majority of the group are Cuban, but it includes several undersignated foreigners. This is the first group of five thousand guerrillas who are reported to be sent to various Latin American countries during 1966.

3F

[Collectors Comment: Another source quoted as saying that "Che" Guevara allegedly was in Bolivia heading a force of guerrillas in the Andes Mountains.]

- end -

Document 18. CIA report stating that Guevara is on his way to Bolivia (April 23, 1966)
1966: CIA document of April 23, 1966, titled "Revolutionary Group Allegedly Bound For Bolivia" states that "Cuban-trained revolutionaries" are going to Bolivia and that Che Guevara is leading a force of guerillas in the Andes.

1967 MAR 17 AM 7 57

INCOMING TELEGRAM
Department of State

SUBJECT: REPORTED GUERILLA ACTIVITY IN BOLIVIA

1. At urgent request of President Barrientos, I called on him at his house this afternoon accompanied by [UNCLEAR] and DEFATT to find him in a meeting with Acting Chief of Armed Forces General Belmonte; Army Commander General LaFuente; Army Chief of Staff Colonel Vasquez; and aides.

2. Barrientos said Bolivian Authorities yesterday morning picked up two guerilla suspects (Vincente Rocaboado Terrazas and Pastor Barrera Quntel) near Ipita, Department of Santa Cruz, coordinates approximately 19 degrees, 40 minutes south and 63 degrees, 32 minutes west.

3. [UNCLEAR] Interrogation in La Paz today, suspects reportedly admitted association with group of guerillas numbering 30 to 40 in region surrounding Ipita, running roughly from Monteagudo and Lagunillas in the South to Valle Grande in the north. They reportedly said group was led by Castroite Cubans and included Peruvians, Argentines and perhaps other foreigners. Suspects reportedly independently identified as also involved with guerillas Moises, Guevara, and person known as "Chino", also recently reported from here BLOCKED OUT as involved in guerilla preparations.

4. Unspecified quantities and types of arms; and had "ample" funds. Suspects were in fact picked up after arousing suspicions of local authorities because of unduly generous offers they were making for food supplies. Proximate cause of their detention may have been however their sale of a .22 caliber rifle.

5. There has been no armed or other type of contact in area with the reported guerillas, although two squads of Bolivian

Document 19. Telegram to Department of State reporting capture of two guerillas and request by President of Bolivia for military aid (March 17, 1967)
Amb. Henderson informs Washington that two guerillas after capture were interrogated, and claimed Che was their leader, but had never seen him. President Barrientos requests aid, and Henderson recommends providing radio locator equipment that Barrientos requested.

ARVECTROOPS are reportedly trailing one-half day behind
elements of them through very difficult terrain.

6. Barrientos and his senior military commanders appeared
   prepared to believe there was some kind of guerilla
   preparation in the area and asserted as a fact there were
   a number of guerilla radio transmitters sending coded
   signals within the region.

7. Barrientos said he believed the guerillas' purpose was to
   divert Bolivian military forces to this remote, densely
   covered and militarily extremely difficult terrain,
   leaving vial centers such as La Paz, Cochabamba, Oruro,
   and the mines with reduced protection against possible
   subversive action in those places.

8. Barrientos said he would not fall in any such trap but
   plans to put security forces in key centers on extra
   alert and send small specially qualified forces into the
   reported guerilla area to "box them in".

9. Barrientos requested immediate assistance from US in
   following respects:

   Jam provision of radio locating equipment and necessary
   technical bank-up to enable GOB to pinpoint reported
   guerilla radio transmitters.

   B. Additional communications equipment which would be
   needed by field forces operating there.

10. Barrientos said he thought security forces in Paraguay
    and Argentina should know of the foregoing in the event
    the reported guerillas are forced out and CWEE in their
    direction. He asked our cooperation in transmitting this
    message.

11. I made no commitments beyond a promise to look into what
    we might be able to do.

12. We are taking this report of guerilla activity with
    some reserve, but see no harm in embassies Asuncion
    and Buenos Aires passing message mentioned paragraph 7
    above, at their discretion.

13. Meanwhile we are seeing what we can do locally about
    providing radio locater equipment before calling for
    further USG help in this regard.

GP-. HENDERSON

Document 19 contd.

163. Editorial Note from Dept. of State publication, *Foreign Relations 1964-1968 South and Central America*

On March 16, 1967, the Embassy in La Paz reported that President Barrientos had personally informed Ambassador Henderson that two guerrilla suspects had been detained by Bolivian authorities ad, upon interrogation, had admitted association with a group of 30 to 40 guerrillas "led by Castroite Cubans" and other foreigners. The suspects reportedly mentioned that Che Guevara was leader of the guerrilla group, but they had not seen him. Barrientos urgently requested U.S. communications equipment to enable the Bolivian Government to locate reported guerrilla radio transmitters. Henderson made no commitments beyond a promise to look into what the United States could do. (Telegram 2314 from La Paz, March 16; National Archives and Records Administration, RG 59, Central Files 1967-69, POL 23-9 BOL)

A year earlier there were intelligence reports that Che Guevara as in South America, but U.S. analysts found little supporting evidence. In a March 4, 1966, memorandum concerning rumors of Guevara's presence in Colombia, FitzGerald noted that "penetrations of insurgent groups had revealed no indication of Guevara's presence in any of these groups." (Central Intelligence Agency, DDO/IMS, Operational Group, Job 78-5505, Area Activity-Cuba) Further analysis by the Agency identified seven conflicting rumors of Guevara's whereabouts. A March 23, 1966, memorandum prepared in the Western Hemisphere Division noted that Guevara's usefulness had been reduced to his ability as a guerrilla, and that "with his myth he is ten feet tall; without it, he is a mortal of normal stature." Under the circumstances, the Agency concluded:

"...it is not believed justifiable to divert considerable amounts of time, money and manpower to an effort to locate Guevara. It is considered far more important to use these assets to penetrate and monitor Communist subversive efforts wherever they may occur, since Guevara's presence in an area will not affect greatly the outcome of any given insurgent effort." (Ibid.)

On March 24, 1967, the Embassy in La Paz reported that Barrientos met with the Deputy Chief of Mission on March 23 to advise him that the guerrilla situation had worsened and that this deterioration caused him increasing concern. Barrientos believed the guerrilla activity was "part of a large subversive movement led by Cuban and other foreigners." He pointed out that Bolivian troops in the area of guerrilla activity were "green and ill-equipped," and reiterated his urgent request for U.S. assistance. The Embassy told Barrientos that "our military officers were working iwth the Bolivian military to ascertain facts relating to requirements." (Telegram 2381 from La Paz, March 24; National Archives and Records Administration, RG 59, Central Files 1967-69, POL 23-9 BOL) Two U.S. military assistance advisory group officers reported that on March 23 guerrillas had ambushed a 22-man Bolivian Army patrol near Nancuahazu, prompting the Embassy to report to the Department on March 27: "There is now sufficient accumulation of information to bring Country Team to accept as fact that there is guerrilla activity in area previously mentioned, that it could constitute potential security threat to GOB." (Telegram 2384 from La Paz, March 27; ibid.)

In a 90-minute meeting with Ambassador Henderson on March 27, Barrientos appealed for direct U.S. budgetary support for the Bolivian armed forces to meet the "emergency and one in which Bolivia was 'helping to fight for the U.S.'"

Document 20. Dept. of State publication, *Foreign Relations 1964-1968 South and Central America, Editorial note 163* describing U.S. meetings concerning "subversion" with President of Bolivia (March–May, 1967)

In reporting this discussion to the Department, Henderson observed:
"I suspect that Barrientos is beginning to suffer some genuine anguish over the sad spectacle offered by the poor performance of his armed forces in this episode; i.e., an impetuous foray into reported guerrilla country, apparently based on a fragment of intelligence and resulting in a minor disaster, which further tended to panic the GOB into a lather of ill-coordinated activity, with less than adequate professional planning and logistical support." Henderson continued, "pressed by his military he may seek resort to the lobbying talents of Ambassador Sanjines in Washington in an effort to end-run proper channels of communication with U.S. authorities." (Telegram 2405 from La Paz, March 29; ibid.)

On march 29, the CIA reported that to guerrillas captured by the Bolivian Army had furnished information that the guerrilla movement "is an independent, international operation under Cuban direction and is not affiliated with any Bolivian political party. The Agency had received information about the development of other guerrilla groups in Bolivia. "Should these other groups decide to go into action at this time, the Bolivian Government would be sorely taxed to cope with them" in addition to the Cuban-backed group. (Memorandum from [name not declassified] to the Chief, Western Hemisphere Division, March 29, Central Intelligence Agency, DDO/IMS, Job 88-01415R, [file name not declassified]

On March 31, the Department responded to Henderson's concerns: "We have no evidence 'end runs' being attempted here." The Department instructed the embassy in La Paz:

According to the CIA report, May 10, Che Guevara told [text not declassified] that he had come to Bolivia "in order to begin a guerrilla movement that would spread to other parts of Latin America." (CIA Information Cable TDCS 314/06486-67; ibid.)

"You may at your discretion inform Barrientos that we most reluctant consider supporting significantly enlarged army, either thru provision additional material or thru renewal budget support. We fully support concept of providing limited amounts of essential material assist carefully orchestrated response to threat, utilizing to maximum extent possible best trained and equipped troops available. Should threat definitely prove greater than capacity present forces, Barrientos can be assured U.S. willingness consider further assistance." (Telegram 166701 to La Paz, March 31; National Archives and Records Administration, RG 59, Central Files 1967-69, POL 23-9 BOL)

Also on March 31, the Department informed U.S. posts in neighboring countries to Bolivia that the current plan "is to block guerrilla escape then bring in, train and prepare ranger-type unit to eliminate guerrillas." The Department also indicated that the United States was considering a special military training team (MTT) "for accelerated training counter guerrilla force." (Telegram 16641 to Buenos Aires, et al., March 31; ibid.)

On May 11 Rostow reported to President Johnson that "CIA has received the first credible report that 'Che' Guevara is alive and operating in South America." The information had come from interrogation of guerrillas captured in Bolivia. "We need more evidence before concluding that Guevara is operational-and not dead, as the intelligence community, with the passage of time, has been more and more inclined to believe." (Memorandum from Rostow to Johnson, May 11; Johnson Library, National Security File, Country File, Bolivia, Vol. IV, Memoranda, January 1966-December 1968)

Document 20 contd.

I. Information submitted follows closely the format of BLOCKED OUT

1. (A4) After diminishing reports of guerilla activity during the weekend of 17-21 March 1967, on 23 March a Bolivian army patrol clashed with a guerilla group ranging in reported numbers from 50-400. This action occurred in NANCAHAUSU (1930S/6340W) area which is located in the southern part of BOLIVIA, approximately 70 kilometers north of CAIRI (2003S/6331W). Information available indicates that the guerilla group consists of approximately 80 percent Bolivians (total strength not over 100), the remainder being Castroite Cubans, Peruvians, Argentineans, and Europeans. They are a well organized force and are armed with modern weapons and under the direction of Castroite Cubans. The Bolivian Army established a forward command post at LAGUNILLAS (1936S/6341W) under the command of the 4th Division. To search out the guerillas the Bolivian Army started with 100 men from the 4th Division stationed at LAGUNILLAS and were later backed by one company consisting of 100 men from the CITE Regiment (US MAP supported) which was airlifted from COCHABAMBA. One company from 8th Division consisting of 100 men from SANTA CRUZ was airlifted to reinforce the 4th Division and two companies consisting of approximately 160-170 men from 2d Regiment "Bolivar" at VIACHA were airlifted to SANTA CRUS and later moved to the CAMIRI area to provide additional strength in the combat area. The Bolivian Army has approximately 600 men involved at the present time in the search for the guerilla band. They are being supported by the Air Force which is providing airlift transportation, strafing and bombing, and aerial reconnaissance of the area. The Bolivian Armed Forces have performed well in the face of this insurgent condition, however, lack of sufficient training, communications, field rations and vehicular transportation has definitely hampered their operations.

2. (c.) Military/Political Affairs.

a. (C1) Role of military in national affairs: The influence of Bolivian military on national policy has been extensive since the coup in November 1964. Traditionally the Bolivian military has always been involved in political affairs and from 4 November 1964 until 6 August 1966 they actually ran the Junta Government and effectively maintained internal security. Their prestige among the population has been excellent. Their work with the populace on civic action projects has gained the understanding, respect and friendship of the people. The Armed Forces insistence on holding early constitutional elections and returning ... the troops to the barracks, which they did, has elevated their position in the

---

Document 21. Dept. of Defense Intelligence Information Report on guerilla activity in March 1967 (March 31, 1967)

This report from Department of Defense assesses Bolivian counterinsurgency capabilities in the face of increasing guerilla activities. It reports a clash between 50 to 400 organized, well-armed guerillas under the direction of Castroite Cubans. U.S. is the only country providing military aid, although Argentina may help us as well.

eyes of the civil populace to an all time high. The Armed Forces have been and are very much concerned about conditions within the country. This is the reason they revolted against the government on 4 November 1964. They have loyally supported the Military Junta and they selected and supported General BARRIENTOS in his campaign for the presidency. They will continue to support General BARRIENTOS and his new government as long as it is honestly and successfully working for the social and economic development of Bolivia. They are in a position as the power behind the throne and are ready if they should ever find the need to step back into the political arena. There have been and there always will be small cliques within the Armed Forces, but generally speaking, as a collective group they do not belong to, nor support, a single political party as such. The Armed Forces as a whole are pro-United States and anti-Communistic. Authority of key political officers in the military is strong since it runs from the President of the country to the Commander of the Armed Forces who also served as President for a short while.

b. (C2) Instability: At the movement the present guerilla activity has had no real detrimental effect against the Armed Forces, however if they fail to control and eliminate the current guerilla threat this situation could change. Although improperly equipped and trained for guerilla warfare, the Armed Forces are performing reasonably well in the current operation. As long as the Armed Forces remain united no current opposition forces, or any combination of forces, should be able to pose a real threat to the security of the country.

c. (C3) Military Assistance: The United States is the only foreign country providing military assistance in hardware to Bolivia. However, Argentina has indicated that it may give Bolivia support in arms and munitions to help in the current guerilla operation, but they will coordinate this with the United States to eliminate duplication. The Bolivian military receives some training in schools in Brazil, Argentina, Peru, Uruguay, and England. Also Argentina has a small Naval Mission in Bolivia which so far has provided only training to the Bolivian Navy. For further details see IR 2 808 120 66, subject: Foreign Military Assistance, dated 31 October 1966.

d. (C4) Collective military agreements: There are no known military agreements between Bolivia and neighboring countries. Bolivia is a member of the Inter-American Defense Board. In addition, it is a signatory of the Rio ILLEGIBLE [end...]

Document 21 contd.

MEMORANDUM OF UNDERSTANDING CONCERNING
THE ACTIVATION, ORGANIZATION AND TRAINING
of the 2d RANGER BATTALION – BOLIVIAN ARMY

PREFACE: Based on an exchange of notes signed at La Paz (Annex A) April 26, 1962. The Government of the United States of America agreed to make available to the Government of Bolivia defense articles and defense services for internal security, subject to the Foreign Assistance Act of 1961. Recognizing a possible threat to the internal security of the Republic of Bolivia in the Oriente, specifically the 3d, 4th, 5th, and 8th Division areas of responsibility, it is agreed that a rapid reaction force of battalion size capable of executing counterinsurgency operations in jungle and difficult terrain throughout this region will be created in the vicinity of Santa Cruz, Republic of Bolivia.

1. Terms of Cooperation.

a. The Bolivian Armed Forces agree to provide a cuartel whose environs include, as a minimum, suitable training areas and facilities for maneuvering of tactical units and the combat firing of all organic weapons; additionally, buildings and shelter will be provided to insure adequate storage, protection, and maintenance of MAP supplied equipment.

b. The Bolivian Armed Forces agree to assign personnel to this unit in the numbers and talents indicated at Annex. B. The reassignment of personnel from or within this unit will be minimal, and their period of service will be not less than two years.

c. The Bolivian Armed Forces agree to furnish initial sufficient quantities of training ammunition to this unit out of it on-hand stocks of MAP and non-MAP ammunition.

d. The Bolivian Armed Forces agree to maintain all U.S. supplied equipment at the highest degrees of combat readiness. This includes technical maintenance as well as such "soft goods" as tires, batteries, lubricants, cleaning and preserving materials in reasonable and adequate quantities. Verification that these standards are met will be accomplished within the terms of Paragraph 6 "Exchange of notes" (Annex A) for recurring inspections made jointly by U.S.-Bolivian army representatives. Additionally equipment status reports will be rendered by the unit commander

22. Contractual Agreement between U.S. Army and Bolivian Army entitled *Memorandum of Understanding Concerning the Activation, Organization, and Training of the 2d Ranger Battalion-Bolivian Army* **(April 28, 1967)**
    This is one of the key documents demonstrating the U.S. deep involvement in the pursuit of Che. It sets forth the agreement by the United States to train and supply soldiers provided by the Bolivian government to pursue and eliminate the guerillas.

to U.S. Army Section/MILGP through 4th Dept. Bolivian Army on a bi-monthly basis.

e. For purposes of identification, the U.S. Army section-MILGP recognizes this unit as the Second Ranger Battalion. This in no way precludes the Bolivian Army from designating this unit by any historical or traditional name that it might desire.

f. The U.S. Army Section-MILGP agrees to equip this unit as rapidly as possible in accordance with the equipment list shown at Annex D. This equipment to be provided within the terms of "Exchange of Notes" 22 April 1962 (sic) (Annex A)

g. The U.S. Army Section-MILGP agrees to support the maintenance of U.S-provided equipment with reasonable quantities of spare and replacement parts, through established logistical channels of the Bolivian Army. It is recognized that the duration of this support will be in accordance with any future modifications of the U.S. Foreign Assistance Act of 1961.

h. The U.S. Army Section-MILGP agrees to provide advisor effort on a continuing basis in both technical and operational areas within its capabilities. Additionally, it will receive requests for special training assistance not locally available.

i. The U.S. Army Section-MILGP will initiate actions, e.g., as soon as an adequate site has been established and personnel have been provided.

2. Recognizing a request from the Armed Forces of Bolivia for special training assistance during the initial organization and training phase of this unit, there will be provided a training team of U.S. Specialists from the 8th Special Forces, a U.S. Army Forces, Panama, C.Z., within the following conditions:

a. The team shall consist of specialists, ranger-qualified, and combat experienced.

b. The team will consist of 16 officers and noncommissioned officers, commanded by an officer not less than the grade of Major. (Team strength to be modified as needed.)

c. The mission of this team shall be to produce a rapid reaction force capable of counterinsurgency operations and skilled to the degree that four months of intensive training can be absorbed b the personnel presented by the Bolivian Armed Forces.

Document 22 contd.

d. The program of training to be presented will be as shown at Annex E.

e. The members of this team will enjoy the same responsibilities, rights, and privileges as afforded other U.S. Army Mission members in Bolivia.

f. The members of this team will not exercise command authority over any member of the Bolivian Armed Forces. However, it is expected that in any training situation, their instructions will be accepted and followed in a spirit of understanding and mutual cooperation. Any misunderstanding arising from these training situations which cannot be resolved by the unit commander and the team chief will be referred to Chief USARSEC and the Army Commander.

g. All members of this Special Training Team are specifically prohibited from participating in actual combat operations either as observers or advisors iwth members of the Bolivian Armed Forces.

h. All members of this Special Training Team are under the operational control of the Chief USARSEC. Any incidents requiring disciplinary action will be referred to Chief USARSEC for necessary action.

3. Wilful disregard, in whole or in part, or these generally stated agreements by either party will in fact nullify this memorandum of understanding.

KENNETH T. MACEK
Colonel, GS
Chief USARSEC/MILGP [?]

DAVID LAGUENTE
Commander
Bolivian Army

ALFREDO OVANDO C
General
Commander, Armed Forces

*Annexes not provided.

Document 22 contd.

THE WHITE HOUSE
WASHINGTON

Thursday - May 11, 1967

Mr. President:

_____ the first credible report that "Che" Guevara is
alive and operating in South America.

We need more evidence before concluding that Guevara is operational -- and not dead, as the intelligence community, with the
passage of time, has been more and more inclined to believe.

Rostow

Attachment

SANITIZED
E.O. 12356. Sec. 3.4
NIJ ___91-32___
By _____, NARA, Date _1-7-93_

Document 23. White House note from Walt Rostow, Special Assistant for National Security Affairs, to President Johnson reporting Che operating in South America (May 11, 1967)

This note on White House stationery from Rostow, the Special Assistant for National Security Affairs to the President demonstrates that Che was being tracked at the highest level of the U.S. government.

Foreign Relations 1964-1968 South and Central America, Editorial Note 164

164. Memorandum From the President's Special Assistant (Rostow) to President Johnson/1/

Washington, June 23, 1967

/1/Source: Johnson Library, National Security File, Country File, Bolivia, Vol. IV, Memoranda, January 1966-December 1968. Secret; Sensitive. The memorandum indicates President Johnson saw it.

Mr. President:

This is what is going on with guerillas in Bolivia:

Last March 24 Bolivian security forces were ambushed in a remote area of southeastern Bolivia as they were investigating reports of a guerilla training camp. Since then 6 other skirmishes have been fought. The Bolivian forces have come off poorly in these engagements, losing 28 of their men to 2 or 3 known rebels killed.

Interrogation of several deserters and prisoners, including a young French communist - Jules Debray - closely associated with Fidel Castro and suspected of serving as a Cuban courier, strongly suggests that the guerillas are Cuban-sponsored, although this is hard to document. There is some evidence that "Che" Guevara *may* have been with the group. Debray reports seeing him. A highly sensitive source [*less than 1 line of source text not declassified*] reports a recent statement by Brezhnev that Guevara is in Latin America "making his revolutions". /2/

/2/ In a June 4 cable to President Johnson, Rostow noted that "CIA believes that 'Che' Guevara has been with this group." He also indicated that "we have put Bolivia on top of this list more because of the fragility of the political situation and the weakness of the armed forces than the size and effectiveness of the guerilla movement." (Ibid., Latin America, Vol. VI, June-September 1967) The CIA received information, reportedly based on a document written and signed by Che Guevara, in which the revolutionary stated that "revolt started in Bolivia because wide-spread discontent there and disorganization army." [*text not declassified*] Central Intelligence Agency, DDo/IMS Files, [*file name not declassified*]

Document 24. *Foreign Relations 1964-1968 South and Central America, Editorial note 164* describing for President Johnson the results of the interrogation of captured French "communist" Regis Debray and others (June 23, 1967)
    Rostow tells President Johnson that Che is in Bolivia, that political situation is fragile and that Bolivian army is weak. He reports that the U.S. has sent a special training team and equipment to help organize a battalion as fast as possible.

Estimates of the strength of the guerillas range from 50 to 60 men. It appears that they were flushed out while still in a preliminary training phase and before they intended to open operations. Despite this, they have so far clearly out-classed the Bolivian security forces. The performance of the government units has revealed a serious lack of command coordination, officer leadership and troop training and discipline.

Soon after the presence of guerillas had been established, we sent a special team and some equipment to help organize another Ranger-type Battalion. On the military side, we are helping about as fast as the Bolivians are able to absorb our assistance. The diversion of scarce resources to the Armed Forces could lead to budgetary problems, and our financial assistance may be needed later this year.

The outlook is not clear. The guerillas were discovered early before they were able to consolidate and take the offensive. The pursuit by the government forces, while not very effective, does keep them on the run. These are two pluses.

At their present strength the guerillas do not appear to pose an immediate threat to Barrientos. If their forces were to be quickly augmented and they were able to open new fronts in the near future, as now rumored, the thin Bolivian armed forces would be hard-pressed and the fragile political situation would be threatened. The hope is that with our help Bolivian security capabilities will out-distance guerilla capabilities and eventually clear them out.

State, DOD, and CIA are following developments closely. /3/ As I mentioned, Defense is training and equipping additional forces. CIA has increased its operations.

/3/ A June 14 memorandum prepared b the CIA focused on Cuban sponsorship of the Bolivian guerillas and the failure of the Bolivian Government to meet the insurgent threat. (Johnson Library, National Security File, Intelligence File, Guerilla Problem in Latin America).

The Argentines and Brazilians are also watching this one. Argentina is the only other country with a military mission in La Paz. Close military ties between Argentina and Bolivia are traditional. The Argentines have also furnished military supplies to the Bolivians.

W.W. Rostow /4/

/4/ Printed from a copy that bears this typed signature

Document 24 contd.

Foreign Relations 1964-1968
South and Central America , Editorial note 165

165. Memorandum of Conversation/1/

Washington, June 29, 1967.

/1/ Source: Johnson Library, National Security File, Country FIle, Bolivia, Vol. IV, Memoranda, January 1966-December 1968. Secret. Prepared by Bowdler. Copies provided to Rostow and Sayre.

PARTICIPANTS
Ambassador of Bolivia
Julio Sanjines-Goytia

Mr. William G. Bowdler

At the invitation of the Bolivian Ambassador, I went to his residence this afternoon to discuss the Bolivian situation.

Most of the one-hour conversation was a monologue by the loquacious Ambassador describing the background to the Barrientos administration and the present political situation. Toward the end of the conversation, he got around to the two points he had on his mind.

The first was increased external assistance. I asked him what specifically he had in mind. He replied that he was not thinking of budgetary support since Bolivia had passed that stage and was proud of its accomplishment. I then asked him what type of project assistance he had in mind. On this he was very vague, saying that we should send a special mission from Washington to study what additional projects might be started to further Bolivia's development.

The question in which he was most interested - and obviously the main purpose for the invitation - was to ask for our help in establishing what he called a "hunter-killer" team to ferret out guerillas. He said this idea was not original with him, but came from friends of his in the CIA. I asked him whether the Ranger Battalion now in training were not sufficient. He said that what he has in mind is 50 to 60 young army officers , with sufficient intelligence, motivation and drive, who could be trained quickly and could be counted on to search out the guerillas with tenacity and courage. I asked him whether such an elite group would

Document 25. *Foreign Relations 1964-1968 South and Central America, Editorial note 165,* Memorandum from William G. Bowdler, staff member of National Security Council, describing request by Bolivian ambassador for a "'hunter-killer' team to ferret out guerillas." (June 29, 1967)

not cause problems within the army and perhaps even political problems between Barrientos and his supporters. The Ambassador said that these problems could be minimized by rotating a fixed number of the team back into the army at regular intervals. The rotation system would have the added benefit of bringing a higher degree of professionalism into the officer ranks of the army. I told him that his idea may have merit, but needs further careful examination.

Before leaving, I told him that I had seen reports that Bolivia might be considering declaring a state of war against Cuba. I asked him whether he had any information to substantiate these reports. He expressed complete surprise and strong opposition, pointing out that such action would expose Bolivia to international ridicule. He speculated that these reports might have been planted by Cuban exiles. He sAid that some Cubans had approached him along this line and there may be Cuban exiles in Bolivia ho are doing likewise with other Bolivian officials. I told him that I also thought that this action would be a serious mistake not only because of the light in which it would cast Bolivia, but also because of the serious legal and practical problems which would arise from being in a state of war with Cuba.

Upon departing, he said he appreciated having the opportunity to talk frankly with me and expressed the desire to exchange views on his country from time to time. I told him I would be happy to do this whenever he thought it useful.

WGB

Document 25 contd.

In a July 5, 1967, memorandum to Special Assistant Walt Rostow, William Bowdler of the National Security Council Staff summarized the current U.S. military training role in Bolivia: "DOD is helping train and equip a new Ranger Battalion. The Bolivian absorption capacity being what it is, additional military assistance would not now seem advisable. [3 lines of source text not declassified]" Bowdler recommended that "a variable of the Special Strike Force acceptable to the Country Team be established. It might be part of the new Ranger Battalion." (Johnson Library, National Security File, Intelligence File, Guerilla Problem in Latin America) The Country Team objections were transmitted in Telegram 2291 from La Paz, May 24. The team stated that a strike force would be viewed by the Bolivians as a "magical solution" and a "substitute for hard work and needed reform." (National Archives and Records Administration, RG 59, Central Files 1967-69, POL 23 NOL)

At 4:30 p.m. on July 5 Rostow, Bowdler, and Peter Jessup met in the Situation Room of the White House with representatives of the Department of State including Assistant Secretary of State Covey Oliver, Deputy Assistant Secretary Robert Sayre, and Ambassador Henderson, with William Lang of the Department of Defense, and Desmond FitzGerald and William Broe of the Central Intelligence Agency. The group agreed that a special strike force as not advisable because of the Embassy's objections. They decided that the United States should "concentrate on the training of the Second Ranger Battalion with the preparation of an intelligence unit to be part of the Battalion." They also agreed to look into expansion of the rural police program, prepare contingency plans to cover the possibility of the insurgency getting beyond the control of Barrientos and the Bolivian armed forces, and suggested that Barrientos might need $2-5 million in grant or supporting assistance in the next 2 months to meet budgetary problems resulting from the security situation. (Memorandum of meeting; Johnson Library, National Security File, Latin America, Vol. VI, June 1967-September 1967) The gist of these decisions was relayed to the President in the context of a broader policy for counterinsurgency in Latin America; see Document 61.

U.S. efforts to support the counterinsurgency program in Bolivia against Cuban-led guerillas followed a two-step approach. To help overcome the deficiencies of the Bolivian Army, a 16-man military training team of the U.S. Special Forces was sent to Bolivia to support the Bolivian

Document 26. *Foreign Relations 1964-1968 South and Central America, Editorial note 166,* Memorandum from William Bowdler to Walt Rostow summarizing current U.S. military training of Bolivian soldiers (July 5, 1967)

Document from Bowdler to Rostow summarizes current U.S. military training of Bolivian soldiers. It indicates weaknesses in the Bolivians intelligence-collecting capability. The CIA was formally given responsibility to plan for and provide this. CIA agents Vilolldo and Rodriguez arrived in Bolivia on August 2, 1967 to train Bolivian Rangers in intelligence gathering. They were also ordered to accompany these soldiers into the field and told to "actually help in directing operations." These assignments were approved by Bolivian President Barrientos, U.S. Ambassador Henderson, and the head of the Bolivian army General Ovando.

Second Ranger Battalion in the development of anti-guerilla tactics and techniques. The United States also provided ammunition, ratios, and communications equipment on an emergency basis under MAP and expedited delivery of four helicopters. (Paper by W.D. Broderick, July 11; National Archives and Records Administration, RG 59, ARA Files: Lot 70 D 443, POL 23-4, 1967, IRG Counter-Insurgency Subgroup) A July 3 memorandum prepared by the CIA reads: "Although original estimates were that the battalion would no be combat ready until approximately December 1967, the MILGROUP now believes that this date can be advanced to mid-September 1967." (Central Intelligence Agency, Job 88-01415R, DDO/IMS, [file name not declassified]

As the training of the Ranger battalion progressed, weaknesses in tis intelligence-collecting capability emerged. The CIA was formally given responsibility for developing a plan to provide such a capability on July 14 (ARG/ARA/COIN Action Memo #1, July 20; National Archives and Records Administration, RG 59, ARA Files, Lot 70 D 122, IRG/ARA/COIN Action Memos) The planned operation was approved by the Department of State, CINCSO, the U.S. Ambassador in La Paz, Bolivian President Barrientos and Commander-in-Chief of the Bolivian Armed Forces Ovando. A team of two instructors arrived in La Paz on August 2. In addition to training the Bolivians in intelligence-collection techniques, the instructors [text not declassified] planed to accompany the Second Ranger battalion into the field. Although the team as assigned in an advisory capacity, CIA "expected that they will actually help in directing operations." The Agency also contemplated this plan "as a pilot program for probable duplication in other Lain American countries faced with the problem of guerilla warfare." (Memorandum for the Acting Chief, Western Hemisphere Division, August 22; ibid.)

Document 26 contd.

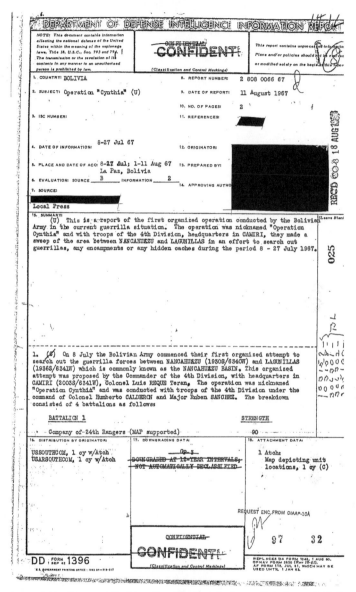

Document 27. Dept. of Defense Intelligence Information Report of the first operation conducted by the Bolivian army against the guerillas (August 11, 1867)

Report from Dept. of Defense of the first operation conducted by the Bolivian army against the guerillas code-named "Operation Cynthia." The report observes "for the first time, upon being fired at, they did not drop their weapons and run." This was the result of U.S. training.

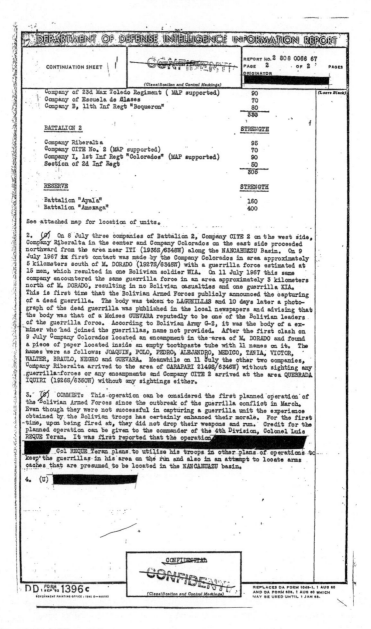

CONTINUATION SHEET

~~CONFIDENTIAL~~

(Classification and Control Markings)

REPORT NO. 2 808 0066 67
PAGE 2 OF 2 PAGES
ORIGINATOR

(Leave Blank)

Company of 23d Max Toledo Regiment (MAP supported)	90
Company of Escuela de Blases	70
Company B, 11th Inf Regt "Boqueron"	80
	336

BATTALION 2	STRENGTH
Company Riberalta	95
Company CITE No. 2 (MAP supported)	70
Company I, 1st Inf Regt "Colorado" (MAP supported)	90
Section of 2d Inf Regt	50
	305

RESERVE	STRENGTH
Battalion "Ayala"	150
Battalion "Amexaga"	400

See attached map for location of units.

2. (C) On 8 July three companies of Battalion 2, Company CITE 2 on the west side, Company Riberalta in the center and Company Colorados on the east side proceeded northward from the area near ITI (1936S/6345W) along the NANCAHUAZU Basin. On 9 July 1967 ix first contact was made by the Company Colorados in area approximately 5 kilometers south of M. DORADO (1927S/6345W) with a guerrilla force estimated at 15 men, which resulted in one Bolivian soldier WIA. On 11 July 1967 this same company encountered the same guerrilla force in an area approximately 3 kilometers north of M. DORADO, resulting in no Bolivian casualties and one guerrilla KIA. This is first time that the Bolivian Armed Forces publicly announced the capturing of a dead guerrilla. The body was taken to LAGUNILLAS and 10 days later a photograph of the dead guerrilla was published in the local newspapers and advising that the body was that of a Moises GUEVARA reputedly to be one of the Bolivian leaders of the guerrilla force. According to Bolivian Army G-2, it was the body of a ex-miner who had joined the guerrillas, name not provided. After the first clash on 9 July Company Colorados located an encampment in the area of M. DORADO and found a piece of paper located inside an empty toothpaste tube with 11 names on it. The names were as follows; JOAQUIN, POLO, PEDRO, ALEJANDRO, MEDICO, TANIA, VICTOR, WALTER, BRAULO, NEGRO and GUEVARA. Meanwhile on 11 July the other two companies, Company Riberalta arrived to the area of CARAPARI 2149S/6346W) without sighting any guerrilla forces or any encampments and Company CITE 2 arrived at the area QUEBRADA IQUIRI (1926S/6350W) without any sightings either.

3. (C) COMMENT: This operation can be considered the first planned operation of the Bolivian Armed Forces since the outbreak of the guerrilla conflict in March. Even though they were not successful in capturing a guerrilla unit the experience obtained by the Bolivian troops has certainly enhanced their morale. For the first time, upon being fired at, they did not drop their weapons and run. Credit for the planned operation can be given to the commander of the 4th Division, Colonel Luis REQUE Teran. It was first reported that the operation

Col REQUE Teran plans to utilize his troops in other plans of operations to keep the guerrillas in his area on the run and also in an attempt to locate arms caches that are presumed to be located in the NANCAHUAZU basin.

4. (U)

~~CONFIDENTIAL~~

~~CONFIDENTIAL~~

(Classification and Control Markings)

DD FORM 1396c
GOVERNMENT PRINTING OFFICE : 1964 O—745193

REPLACES DA FORM 1048-1, 1 AUG 60
AND DA FORM 606, 1 AUG 60 WHICH
MAY BE USED UNTIL 1 JAN 65.

Document 27 contd.

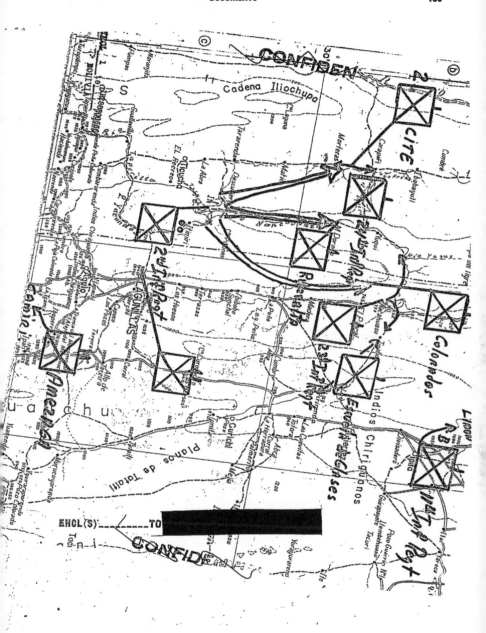

Document 27 contd.

CONFIDENTIAL
Department of State ~~EXCISE~~ **TELEGRAM**
F760003-1947 ~~UNCLASSIFIED~~

Pol 23-9 Bil

E 186

~~UNCLASSIFIED~~

PAGE ?1 LA PAZ 00513 050211Z DECLASSIFICATION DATE 2/27/76
PER HRyon OFFICE ARA
FADRC FOI CASE NO. 5-R-143

89
ACTION ARA 19

INFO USIE 00,RSR 01,SP 02,SS 35,GPM 03,SC 01,NSC 10,RSC 01,P 04,

CIA 04,NSAE 00,INR 07,AID 32,EUR 25,NIC 01,PC 04,SAH 03,L 03,

H 02,/155 W

P R 041920Z SEP 67
FM AMEMBASSY LA PAZ
TO SECSTATE WASHDC PRIORITY 2866
INFO AMEMBASSY ASUNCION 113
AMEMBASSY BRASILIA 44
AMEMBASSY BUENOS AIRES 203
AMEMBASSY LIMA 323
AMEMBAOMY MONTEVIDEO 96
AMEMBASSY PARIS 36
AMEMBASSY RIO DE JANEIRO 175
AMEMBASSY SANTIAGO 172
AMCONSUL COCHABAMBA UNN
USCINCSO
DOD

DEPARTMENT OF STATE A/CDC/MR

REVIEWED by ____ DATE 2-27
( ) RELEASE ( ) DECLASSIFY
( ) EXCISE (X DECLASSIFY in PART
( ) DENY ( ) Non-responsive info.
FOI, EO or PA exceptions ____ (b)(1)
____ S Per Kourtis ____ TS authority to:
(X CLASSIFY as CONFIDENTIAL ____, OADR
( ) DOWNGRADE TS to ( )S or ( )C, OADR

9003572

~~CONFIDENTIAL~~ LA PAZ 513

JOINT EMBASSY/USIS MESSAGE

PAGE 2 RUESLZHNGVIA

SUBJECT: GUERRILLAS

REF: LA PAZ 506

1. PRESENCIA SEPT. 3 CARRIED STORY SANTA CRUZ

~~UNCLASSIFIED~~ ~~UNCLASSIFIED~~

Document 28. Dept. of State telegram concerning interview of wounded guerilla Jose Castillo (Paco) reporting on Debray and Tania (September 4, 1967)

Dept. of State telegram to Secretary of State concerning capture and interview of wounded guerilla Jose Castillo (Paco) who gave information on Debray and Tania. Tania was just killed in combat and the Bolivians were searching for her body. This document like many others demonstrates the hands on role of the highest levels of the U.S. government in eliminating Che.

F780003-1948

Department of State UN TELEGRAM

~~CONFIDENTIAL~~
~~UNCLASSIFIED~~TIAL

PAGE 02 LA PAZ 00513 050211Z

CORRESPONDENT EDWIN CHACON, WHO INTERVIEWED
GUERRILLA JOSE CARILLO, SLIGHTLY WOUNDED AND
CAPTURED AUG. 31 CLASH. CHACON QUOTED CARILLO
AS SAYING QUOTE DEBRAY WAS IN NANCAHUAZU, CARRYING
ARMS AND NEARLY ALWAYS WITH THE GUEVARA AND THE
CUBANS UNQUOTE. CARRILLO ALSO SAID DEBRAY GAVE
LECTURES LP GUERRILLAS BUT HE (CARRILLO) WAS
ON GUARD DUTY AND DID NOT HEARIRHEM. CARRILLO
ALSO REPORTED AS SAYING (A) HE MET GUEVARA WEARING
SPARSE DARD IN NANCAHUAZU DURING FIRST WEEK JANUARY,
(B) GUEVARA PARTICIPATED ATTACK ON SAMAIPATA AND
LEFT ARE SEVERAL DAYS LATER WITH FIVE UNIDENTIFIED

PAGE 3 RUESLZ 038A ▬▬▬▬▬▬▬
CUBANS. (C) TANIA WAS WITH GUERRILLA GROUP FROM
BEGINNING AND WAS VERY VALIANT, (D) HE, CARRILLO,
WAS MEMBER COMMUNIST YOUTH ORGANIZATION ORURO AND
UNEMPLOYED SINCE 1964, JOINED GUERRILLA GROUP
NANCAHUAZU JAN. THIS YEAR WITH TEN OTHER BOLIVIANS,
MET FORTY MORE AT CAMP WHERE RECEIVED ARMS TRAINING,
AND LATER FOUGHT WITH VARIOUS GROUPS.

2. COMMUNIQUE RELEASED LAST NIGHT INDICATED NEW FIRE-
FIGHT OCCURRED SEPT. 3 BETWEEN GUERRILLA FRACTION AND
ELEMENTS FOURTH DIVISION AT PALMARITO. ONE GUERRILLA
KILLED AND BODY TRANSPORTED CAMIRI FOR IDENTIFICATION.
DEFATT CONFIRMS AND STATES NO BAF CASUALTIES.

3 PRESS REPORTS ANOTHER GUERRILLA FRACTION CONTACTED
MORNING SEPT. 3 BY EIGHTH DIVISION UNIT AT MASICURI BAJO
AVADO DE CASOL SHORT DISTANCE FROM SITE AUGUST 31 CLASH.
PRESENCIA CLAIMS FIREFIGHT FOLLOWED THOUGH NO DETAILS YET
AVAILABLE NO OFFICIAL CONFIRMATION.

PAGE 4 RI SLZ 038A ▬▬▬▬▬▬▬ L

4. ARMY COMMANDER LA FUENTE ANNOUNCED MILITARY UNCLASSIFIED

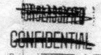

~~UNCLASSIFIED~~

~~CONFIDENTIAL~~

Document 28 contd.

~~CONFIDENTIAL~~

Department of State **TELEGRAM**

F760003-1949

~~UNCLASSIFIED~~

PAGE 03   LA PAZ 00513   050211Z

PATROLS ARE SEARCHING RIO GRANDE FOR BODIES TANIA
AND NEGRO, ALLEGEDLY KILLED AUGUST 31. HOWEVER,
ARMY G-3 INFORMS. DEFATT SINCE BODIES NOT YET
RECOVERED IT IS NOW BELIEVED THEY MAY ALREADY
ESCAPED.

5. COMMENT: ⌐ ¬ CORRECT NAME PRISONER
IS JOSE CASTILLO CHAVEZ (AKA PACO) AND JOINED
GUERRILLAS FEB. NOT JAN. AS REPORTED PRESS. HENDERSON

B]A5

~~UNCLASSIFIED~~ ~~TIAL~~ ~~UNCLASSIFIED~~

~~CONFIDENTIAL~~

Document 28 contd.

34

.... TE CONF OADR

Pel 23-7 Bol
6 Cuba

Department of ~~EXCISE~~
~~CONFIDENTIAL~~ **TELEGRAM**
F760003-1922
~~UNCLASSIFIED~~ UNCLASSIFIED (126) X

PAGE 01 LA PAZ 00826 091939Z DECLASSIFICATION DATE 2/27/74
PER H Ryan OFFICE ARA
48
ACTION ARA 19 FADRC FOI CASE NO. 5-B-143

INFO SSD 00, USIE 00, NSCE 00, CCO 00, SP 02, SS 35, GPM 03, SC 0, NSC 10,

RSC 01, L 03, H 02, SAH 03, EUR 25, P 04, INR 07, CIA 04, NSAE 00, NIC 01

ACDA 17, RSR 01 / 38 W

. . . .

O R 091915Z OCT 67   9003572
FM AMEMBASSY LA PAZ
TO SECSTATE WASHDC IMMEDIATE 3085   DEPARTMENT OF STATE A/CDC/MR
INFO DOD   REVIEWED by   DATE
DIA   ( ) DECLASS   ( ) DECLASSIFY
USCINCSO   ( ) EXCISE   ( ) DECLASSIFY in PART
                                    ( ) DELIY   ( ) Non-responsive info.
                                    FOI, EO or PA exemptions
LA PAZ 826   S. Meskante   TS authority to:
                                    ( ) CLASSIFY as CONFIDENTIAL, OADR
SECDEF FOR OSD/ISA   ( ) DOWNGRADE TS to ( ) S or ( ) C, OADR

SUBJECT: CHE GUEVARA

1. ACCORDING [   ] CHE GUEVARA TAKEN
PRISONER BY BOLIVIAN ARMY UNITS IN HIGUERAS AREA SOUTHWEST   BIAS
OF VILLAGRANDE SUNDAY, OCTOBER 8.

2. GUEVARA RELIABLY REPORTED STILL ALIVE WITH LEG WOUND
IN CUSTODY BOLIVIAN TROOPS IN HIGUERAS MORNING OCTOBER 9.

PAGE 2 RUESLZ 099A
BOLIVIAN ARMY COMMANDER GENERAL DAVID LAFUENTE DEPARTED
LA PAZ FOR GUERRILLA ZONE MORNING OCTOBER 9, PRESUMABLY
TO VERIFY FIRST HAND IDENTITY OF GUEVARA.

GP-4 HENDERSON

~~CONFIDENTIAL~~
~~UNCLASSIFIED~~  UNCLASSIFIED

**Document 29. Dept. of State telegram reporting Che taken prisoner by
Bolivian army and still alive (October 9, 1967)**
   Telegram from U.S. embassy to Sec. of State reporting Che was taken prisoner on
October 8, that he was reliably reported still alive with a leg wound and held by Bolivian
troops in Higueras on morning of October 9, 1967. The missing source is likely CIA
agent Felix Rodriguez.

MEMORANDUM

(14)

THE WHITE HOUSE
WASHINGTON

CONFIDENTIAL

9

Monday, October 9, 1967 -- 6:10 p.m.

Mr. President:

This tentative information that the Bolivians got Che Guevara will interest you. It is not yet confirmed. The Bolivian unit engaged is the one we have been training for some time and has just entered the field of action.

"1.   President Barrientos at 10:00 a.m., October 9, told a group of newsmen, but not for publication until further notice, that Che Guevara is dead.

2.   No further confirmation or details as yet."

"Presencia, October 9, reports capture "Che" Guevara. Guerrillas reported lost three dead and two seriously wounded and captured, including "Che" in six hour firefight on October 8 with unit of 2nd Rangers, seven kilometers north of Higuera. Bolivian armed forces losses two dead and four wounded. General Ovando reportedly proceeding to Vallegrande today at head of investigating team for purpose of identifying guerrilla dead and captured.

"Comment: This confirms Bolivian armed forces conviction that "Che" Guevara earlier seriously wounded or ill and among captured. Among dead are believed to be two Cubans, "Antonio" and "Arturo", not otherwise identified. Also captured is said to be Bolivian "Willy" (identified as Simon Cuba). Due to nightfall, evacuation of dead and wounded guerrillas deferred until morning, October 9. Bolivian armed forces believes Rangers have surrounded guerrilla force boxed into canyon and expect to eliminate them soon."

Walt Rostow

DECLASSIFIED
E.O. 12356, Sec. 3.4
NLJ 91-31
By ____ NARA, Date 7-23-91

Document 30. White House memo from Rostow to President Johnson reporting capture of Che Guevara (October 9, 1967)
    Rostow in note to President Johnson states that Che was captured and brags that the Bolivian unit "engaged is the one we have been training for some time."

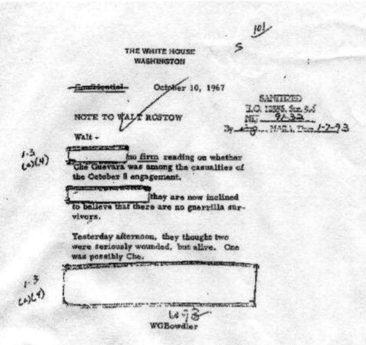

THE WHITE HOUSE
WASHINGTON

~~Confidential~~   October 10, 1967

SANITIZED
E.O. 12356, Sec. 3.4
NLJ ___9/-32___
By ___ NARA, Date 1-2-93

NOTE TO WALT ROSTOW

Walt -

[redacted] no firm reading on whether
Che Guevara was among the casualties of
the October 8 engagement.

[redacted] they are now inclined
to believe that there are no guerrilla survivors.

Yesterday afternoon, they thought two
were seriously wounded, but alive. One
was possibly Che.

[redacted]

WGBowdler

COPY LBJ LIBR...

Document 31. White House memo from Bowdler to Rostow stating that it is not known if Guevara was among the casualties (October 10, 1967)
   White House memo from Bowdler of the National Security Council to Rostow stating that it is not known if Guevara was among the casualties. This note was sent on October 10, a day after Che had been murdered. It was sent after Rostow, basing his information on CIA agent Rodriguez, had reported to the President that Che was taken alive.

MEMORANDUM

THE WHITE HOUSE
WASHINGTON

Wednesday – 10:30 am
October 11, 1967

~~SECRET~~

MEMORANDUM FOR THE PRESIDENT

SUBJECT: Death of "Che" Guevara

SANITIZED
E.O. 12958, Sec. 3.6
NLJ 95-319
By cb , NARA Date 1-8-97

This morning we are about 99% sure that "Che" Guevara is dead. ▓▓▓▓▓▓▓▓▓▓▓▓▓▓▓▓▓▓▓▓▓▓▓▓▓▓▓▓▓▓▓▓▓▓ These should arrive in Washington today or tomorrow.

CIA tells us that the latest information is that Guevara was taken alive. After a short interrogation to establish his identity, General Ovando -- Chief of the Bolivian Armed Forces -- ordered him shot. I regard this as stupid, but it is understandable from a Bolivian standpoint, given the problems which the sparing of French communist and Castro courier Regis Debray has caused them.

The death of Guevara carries these significant implications:

-- It marks the passing of another of the aggressive, romantic revolutionaries like Sukarno, Nkrumah, Ben Bella -- and reinforces this trend.

-- In the Latin American context, it will have a strong impact in discouraging would-be guerrillas.

-- It shows the soundness of our "preventive medicine" assistance to countries facing incipient insurgency -- it was the Bolivian 2nd Ranger Battalion, trained by our Green Berets from June-September of this year, that cornered him and got him.

We have put these points across to several newsmen.

W. Rostow

Document 32. White House memo from Rostow to President Johnson stating that the CIA told Rostow that Guevara was taken alive and ordered shot by the Bolivian army (October 11, 1967)

Memo from Rostow to President Johnson stating that the CIA told Rostow that Guevara was taken alive and ordered shot by the Bolivian army. This is the official U.S. version of Che's murder. Rostow, calls the killing "stupid," but then expands on the positives of having him dead.

MEMORANDUM

THE WHITE HOUSE
Wednesday, 10:30 am
October 1[UNCLEAR], 1967

MEMORANDUM FOR THE PRESIDENT

SUBJECT: Death of "Che" Guevara

This morning we are about 99% sure that "Che" Guevara is dead. [1.5 lines excised] These should arrive in Washington today or tomorrow.

CIA tells us that the latest information is that Guevara was taken alive. After a short interrogation to establish his identity, General Ovando -- Chief of the Bolivian Armed Forced -- ordered him shot. I regard this as stupid, but it is understandable from a Bolivian standpoint, given the problems which the sparing of French communist and Castro courier Regis Debray has caused them.

The death of Guevara carries these significant implications:

-- It marks the passing of another of the aggressive, romantic revolutionaries like Sukarno, Nkrumah, Ben Bella -- and reinforces this trend.

-- In the Latin American context, it will have a strong impact in discouraging would-be guerillas.

-- It shows the soundness of our "preventive medicine" assistance to countries facing incipient insurgency -- it was the Bolivian 2nd Ranger battalion, trained by our Green Berets from June-September of this year that cornered him and got him.

We have put these points across to several newsmen.

Walt Rostow

Document 32 contd. Transcription of original White House memo from Rostrow to President Johnson

US DEPARTMENT OF STATE
Director of Intelligence and Research

TO: The Secretary
THROUGH: S/S
FROM: INR - THOMAS L. HUGHES

SUBJECT: Guevara's Death -- The Meaning for Latin America

"Che" Guevara's death was a crippling - perhaps fatal - blow to the
Bolivian guerilla movement and may prove a serious setback for Fidel
Castro's hopes to foment violent revolution in "all or almost all" Latin
American countries. Those Communists and others who might have been
prepared to initiate Cuban-style guerilla warfare will be discouraged,
at least for a time, by the defeat of the foremost tactician of the
Cuban revolutionary strategy at the hands of one of the weakest armies
in the hemisphere. However, there is little likelihood that Castro
and his followers throughout Latin America will cease tehir efforts
to foment and support insurgency, albeit perhaps with some tactical
modifications.

The mystery of Guevara. Argentina-born Ernesto "Che" Guevara, Fidel
Castro's right-hand man and chief lieutenant in the Sierra Maestra,
author of a book on guerilla tactics, one-time president of Cuba's
National Bank under Castro and later Minister of Industries, mysteriously
disappeared in March 1965. Rumor said that he was ill, or that he has
been put to death by Castro, or that he was in the Dominican Republic
during its civil war or in Vietnam or in the Congo. In October 1965,
Castro finally announced that Guevara had renounced his Cuban citizenship
and set of to devote his services to the revolutionary cause in other
lands. Rumors as to his whereabouts continued, but until recently there
was no substantial evidence to prove even that he was alive.

Guevarismo makes a strong comeback. The March 1965 disappearance of
Guevara occurred during a period when Fidel Castro was toning down his
emphasis on violent revolution and trying to compose his differences
with the traditional pro-Soviet communist parties in Latin America.
But it was not long before Castro again began to favor openly the
independent revolutionary theory which he and Guevara had developed
based on their view of the Cuban revolution. Since the Tricontinental
Conference in Havana in January 1966, Castro has advocated with
increasing stridency the thesis which is set forth most clearly in the
book entitled *Revolution Within the Revolution* by Castro's principal

**Document 33. Dept. of State Intelligence Note, *Guevara's Death-The Meaning
for Latin America* (October 12, 1967)**
     Dept. of State Intelligence Note, *Guevara's Death-The Meaning for Latin America* proves
the importance to the United States of having Che dead. It opens by stating that Che
Guevara's death "was a crippling—perhaps fatal—to the Bolivian guerilla movement and
may prove a serious setback for Fidel Castro's hopes to foment violent revolution."

theoretical apologist, French Marxist intellectual Jules Regis Debray (now on trial in Bolivia). Disgusted with the "peaceful path-to-power" arguments of the Latin American old-line communist parties – especially the Venezuelan CP – and their Soviet supporters, Fidel and Debray have asserted that Latin America is ripe for insurgency now and have specified that the rural guerilla movement rather than any urban-based communist party or other group must be the focal point and the headquarters of the insurgency. They have declared that action must take precedence over ideology and that the guerilla movement -- as the nucleus of a Marxist-Leninist Party – will create the objective conditions for its ultimate success and attract the local peasantry.

On April 17 this year Cuban media gave great play to an article supposedly written by Guevara reiterating the Castro-Guevarist-Debray thesis. Two days later Fidel praised the article and eulogized Guevara, eliminating any lingering impression that the romantic "Che" had been removed from the Cuban pantheon.

LASO Conference highlights disagreement of orthodox communists. The first Latin American Solidarity Organization meeting in Havana this summer served to underscore disagreement with the Castro thesis by the old-line communist parties.

They argue that conditions for violent revolution exist only in very few Latin American countries at present and that the local communist parties – not Cubans or other foreigners – should be the only ones to determine in accordance with traditional Marxist theory what tactics are called for. Despite an outward show of harmony among the delegates, the LASO conference, of which Guevara was named honorary president in absentia, widened the breach between the pro-Moscow communists and those who want revolution now.

Bolivia: testing ground for the theory? The guerilla insurgency in Bolivia which came to light in March 1967 rekindled international interest in Latin American insurgencies and especially in the movements then underway in Latin America. The Guatemalan guerillas seemed to be on the ropes; guerilla forces in Venezuela and Colombia were making no headway. The new Bolivian insurgency, on the other hand, seemed to be the most promising. In an effort to maintain unity with Castro and within the Latin American extreme left, even traditional communist parties agreed to endorse the Bolivian guerillas. Interest was further heightened when in April Debray himself was captured by the Bolivian armed forces and he indicated hat Che Guevara had organized and was leading the guerillas.

Initial battles between the guerillas and the Bolivian army last March and April proved almost disastrous to the poorly trained, ill-equipped

Document 33 contd.

troops who suffered heavy losses in every encounter. The failure of the army to deal effectively with a handful of insurrectionists shook the entire Bolivian government and led to desperate appeals for U.S. assistance. Neighboring counties began to consider what action might be required by them. But the guerillas proved neither invincible nor infallible. By July, aided by testimony from Debray and other captives who were members of the guerila force or had contact with it, as well as by peasants who demonstrated more loyalty to the armed forces than to the guerillas despite the latters' efforts to woo them, Bolivian army units were able to inflict some damage on the guerillas albeit with fairly heavy casualties. In late August, a significant victory took place when the guerila rear guard was wiped out in a well-executed ambush. Still, a successful encounter with the main body of the guerila force did not occur until October 8, when the army recouped is reputation by the action which resulted in the death of Guevara.

Effects in Bolivia. Guevara's death is a feather in the cap of Bolivian President Rene Barrientos. It may signal the end of the guerila movement as a threat to stability. If so, the Bolivian military, which is a major element of Barrientos' support, will enjoy a sense of self-confidence and strength that it has long lacked. However, victory could also stir political ambitions among army officers who were directly involved in the anti-guerilla campaign and who may now see themselves as the saviors of the republic.

Castro's reaction: public rededication and private reassessment. Cuban domestic media have thus far limited their reporting on Guevara's death to mentioning "insistent statements" to this effect in the international press which Cuban authorities can neither confirm nor deny. However, the broad outlines of Havana's public position are generally predictable. Guevara will be eulogized as the model revolutionary who met a heroic death. His exemplary conduct will be contrasted to the do-nothing, cowardly theorizing of the old-line communist parties and other "pseudo-revolutionaries" in Latin America and elsewhere. The Castro-Guevara-Debray thesis will be upheld as still valid and the protracted nature of the struggle will be emphasized. Blame for Guevara's death will be attributed to the usual villains – US imperialism, the Green Berets. the CIA – with only passing contemptuous references to the Bolivian "lackeys". A call will no doubt be made for new "Che's" to pick up the banner of the fallen leader and optimistic predictions will be make as to the inevitability of the final triumph.

In private, however, Castro and his associates will have to reappraise the prospects for exported revolution. Castro might up his commitment

Document 33 contd.

of Cuban men and resources to foreign insurgency in order to demonstrate that the death of one combatant, even the illustrious "Che" – makes little difference to the eventual success of guerilla struggle in the hemisphere. Such response would fit with Casto's characteristic refusal to accept failure in a major undertaking. Or he might curtail Cuba's efforts to foster insurgency abroad, pending further assessment and stocktaking o n the prospects for potential and existing insurgencies. Or, on analyzing the Guevara effort in Bolivia, he might adopt some new tactical approaches for guerilla movements. On balance, it seems most likely that he will continue to commit about the same level of resources as at present to promoting revolutionaries while utilizing the memory of the "martyred" Guevara and perhaps some tactical changes in approach.

Probable Latin American reaction to Guevara's death. News of Guevara's death will relieve most non-leftist Latin Americans who feared that sooner or later he might foment insurgencies in their countries. The demise of the most glamorous and reputedly effective revolutionary may even cause some Latin Americans to downgrade the seriousness of insurgency and the social factors which breed it. On the other hand, communists of whatever stripe and other leftists are likely to eulogize the revolutionary martyr – especially for his contribution to the Cuban revolution – and to maintain that revolutions will continue until their causes are eradicated.

If the Bolivian guerilla movement is soon eliminated as a serious subversive threat, the death of Guevara will have even more important repercussions among Latin American communists. The dominant peaceful line groups, who were either in total disagreement with Castro or paid only lip-service to the guerilla struggle, will be able to argue with more authority against the Castro-Guevara-Debray thesis. They can point out that even a movement led by the foremost revolutionary tactician, in a country which apparently provided conditions suitable for revolution, had failed. While these parties are unlikely to entirely denigrate Che's importance and abilities, they will be able to accuse the Cubans of adventurism and point out that the presence of so many Cubans and other foreigners among the leaders of the Bolivian guerillas tended to alienate the peasants upon whose support they ultimately depended. They will not be able to argue that any insurgency must be indigenous and that only local parties know when local conditions are ripe for revolution. Castro certainly will not be able to disassociate himself from Guevara's Bolivian efforts and will be subject to "we told you so" criticism from the old-line parties. Although leftist groups which may have marginally accepted the Cuban theory probably will reevaluate their policies. Castro's spell on the more youthful leftist elements win the hemisphere will not be broken.

Document 33 contd.

THE WHITE HOUSE
WASHINGTON

~~SECRET~~   Friday - 4:00 pm
October 13, 1967

Mr. President:

This removes any doubt that "Che"
Guevara is dead.

Walt Rostow

Document 34. White House memo from Rostow to Johnson stating "Guevara is dead" (October 13, 1967)
   White House memo from Rostow to Johnson stating that "Guevara is dead." Although several sentences are deleted, the conclusion is likely based on an examination of the fingerprints from Che's severed hands.

172. Memorandum From Director of Central Intelligence Helms/1/

Washington, October 13, 1967

/1/ Source: Johnson Library, National Security File, Country File, Bolivia, Vol. IV, Memoranda, January 1966–December 1968. Secret. Copies of this memorandum in CIA files indicate that it was drafted by Broe and [*name not declassified*] in the Western Hemisphere Division and approved by Karamessines. (Central Intelligence Agency, DDO/IMS, Operational Group, Job 78-06423A, U.S. Government-President)

Memorandum For
The Secretary of State
The Secretary of Defense
Mr. Walt W. Rostow
Assistant Secretary of State for Inter-American Affairs

SUJECT
Statements by Ernesto "Che" Guevara Prior to His Execution in Bolivia

1. Further details have now been obtained from [*less than 1 line of source text not declassified*] who was on the scene in the small village of Higueras where Ernesto "Che" Guevara was taken after his capture on 8 October 1967 b the Bolivian Army's Second Ranger Battalion./2/

/2/ A full account of the capture and death of Che Guevara is in the CIA Intelligence Information Cable [*telegram number not declassified*]

2. [*less than 1 line of source text not declassified*] attempted to interrogate Guevara on 9 October 1967 as soon as he got access to him at around 7 a.m. At that time "Che" Guevara was sitting on the floor in the corner of a small, dark schoolroom, in Higueras. He had his hands over his face. His wrists and feet were tied. In front of him on the floor lay the corpses of two Cuban guerillas. Guevara had a flesh wound in his leg, which was bandaged.

3. Guevara refused to be interrogated but permitted himself to be drawn into a conversation with [*less than 1 line of source text not declassified*] during which he made the following comments:

   a. Cuban economic situation: Hunger in Cuba is the result of

Document 35. *Foreign Relations 1964-1968 South and Central America, Editorial note 172, Memorandum from Director of Central Intelligence Helms to Secretaries of State, Defense and Rostow* giving details of the "capture and death of Che Guevara" (October 13, 1967)

" This was almost surely based on information from CIA agent Felix Rodriguez, and gives the version of the murder that blames the Bolivians and exonerates the United States.

pressure by United States imperialism. Now Cuba has become self-sufficient in meat production and has almost reached the point where it will begin to export meat. Cuba is the only economically self-sufficient country in the Socialist world.

b. Camilo CIenfuegos: For many years the story has circulated that Fidel Castro Ruz had Cienfuegos, one of his foremost deputies, killed because his personal popularity presented a danger to Castro. Actually the death of Cienfuegos was an accident. Cienfuegos had been in Oriente Province when he received a call to attend a general staff meeting in Havana. He left by plane and the theory was that the plane became lost in low-ceiling flying conditions, consumed all of its fuel, and crashed in the ocean, and no trace of him was ever found. Castro had loved Cienfuegos more than any of his lieutenants.

c. Fidel Castro Ruiz: Castro had not been a Communist prior to the success of the Cuban Revolution. Castro's own statements on the subject are correct.

d. The Congo: American imperialism had not been the reason for his failure there but, rather, the Belgian mercenaries. He denied ever having several thousand troops in the Congo, as sometimes reported, but admitted having had "quite a few".

e. Treatment of Guerilla Prisoners in Cuba: During the course of the Cuban Revolution and its aftermath, there had been only about 1,500 individuals killed, exclusive of armed encounters such as the Bay of Pigs. The Cuban Government, of course, executed all guerilla leaders who invaded its territory... (He stopped then with a quizzical look on his face and smiled as he recognized his own position on Bolivian soil.)

f. Future of Guerilla Movement in Bolivia: With his capture, the guerilla movement had suffered an overwhelming setback in Bolivia, but he predicted a resurgence in the future. He insisted that his ideals would win in the end even though he was disappointed at the lack of response from the Bolivian campesinos. The guerilla movement had failed partially because of Bolivian Government propaganda which claimed that the guerillas represented a foreign invasion of Bolivian soil. In spite of the lack of popular response from the Bolivian campesinos, he had not planned on exfiltration route from Bolivia in case of failure. He had definitely decided to either fall or win in this effort.

Document 35 contd.

4. According to [*less than one line of source text not declassified*] when Guevara, Simon Cuba, and Aniceto Reynaga Godillo were captured on 8 October, the Bolivian Armed Forces Headquarters ordered that they be kept alive for a time. A telegraphic code was arranged between La Paz and Higueras with the numbers 500 representing Guevara, 600 meaning the phrase "keep alive" and 700 representing "execute". During the course of the discussion with Guevara, Simon Cuba and Aniceto Reynaga were detained in the next room of the schoolhouse. At one stage, a burst of shots was heard and [*less than 1 line of source text not declassified*] learned later that Simon Cuba had been executed. A little later a single shot was heard and it was learned afterward that Aniceto Reynaga had been killed. When the order came at 11:50 from La Paz to kill Guevara, the execution was delayed as long as possible. However, when the local commander was advised that a helicopter would arrive to recover the bodies at approximately 1:30 p.m., Guevara was executed with a burst of shots at 1:15 p.m. Guevara's last words were, "Tell my wife to remarry and tell Fidel Castro that the Revolution will again rise in the Americas." To his executioner he said, "Remember, you are killing a man."/3/

/3/ The [*text not declassified*] on site, reporting on Guevara's execution, indicated that "it was impossible keep him alive." [*telegram number not declassified*] October 10; ibid., [*file name not declassified*]

5. At no time during the period he was under [*less than 1 line of source text not declassified*] observation did Guevara lose his composure.

Dick/4/

/4/ Printed from a copy that indicates Helms signed the original.

Document 35 contd.

CIA
INTELLIGENCE INFORMATION CABLE

17 October 1967

SUBJECT:
1. Background of Soviet Premier Aleksey Kosygin's visit to Havana
2. Content of discussions between Kosygin and Cuban Premier Fidel Castro

October 1967

SOURCE: BLOCKED

(SUMMARY: [BLOCKED] In late 1966 [BLOCKED] Brezhnev strongly criticized the dispatch of Ernesto "Che" Guevara to Bolivia and Castro's policy with respect to the support of revolutionary activity in Latin America. During Kosygin's visit Castro explained the basis of his revolutionary policy. Cuba evaluated the Kosygin visit as productive, although it was clear that divergent views continued to exist regarding revolutionary activity in Latin America. End summary).

1. [BLOCKED] In the fall of 1966 Castro [BLOCKED] informed Brezhnev that Ernesto "Che" Guevara, with men and material furnished by Cuba, had gone to Bolivia to mount a revolution within that country. [BLOCKED] In June 1967, Brezhnev, in response to a question about Guevara, [one word BLOCKED] replied that he (Guevara) was there in Latin America "Making his revolutions." [BLOCKED] Brezhnev expressed his disappointment at the failure of Castro to give the Soviet Union advance notice concerning the dispatch of Guevara, and in strong terms criticized the decision of Castro to undertake guerilla activities in Bolivia or other Latin American countries. Brezhnev stated that such activities were harmful to the true interests of the communist cause and inquired as to "what right" Castro had to foment revolution in Latin America without appropriate coordination with the other "socialist" countries.

2. [BLOCKED] It appears that Castro was irritated at [BLOCKED] Brezhnev [BLOCKED] the Soviets decided that a visit to Cuba by one of the Soviet leaders was advisable. Plans for the visit had been completed before the Middle East crisis erupted in the spring of 1967. Subsequently, when it was decided that Premier Kosygin would visit the United States to address the United Nations General Assembly concerning the Middle East crisis, it was agreed that Kosygin would return to Moscow via Havana.

3. The primary purpose of Kosygin's trip to Havana 26-30 June 1967 as to inform Castro concerning the Middle East crisis, notably to explain Soviet policy regarding the crisis. A secondary but important reason for the trip was to discuss with Castro the subject of Cuban revolutionary activity in Latin America. [BLOCKED] Kosygin repeated

Document 36. CIA *Intelligence Information Cable* **expressing Soviet Premier Brezhnev's criticism of Che and Fidel's response (October 17, 1967)**
    CIA *Intelligence Information Cable*. Fidel responds to Soviet criticism of Che's guerilla activities by stating that Che had gone to Bolivia as was his right as a "Latin American to contribute to the liberation of his country and the entire continent...."

the Soviet view that Castro was harming the communist cause through his sponsorship of guerilla activity in Latin America and through providing support to various anti-government groups, which although they claimed to be "socialist" or communist, were engaged in disputes with the "legitimate" Latin American communist parties i.e., those favored by the USSR. Kosygin said that the internecine struggles among the various left revolutionary groups were playing into the hands of the imperialists and were weakening and diverting the efforts of the "socialist world" to "liberate" Latin America.

4. In replying to Kosygin Castro [BLOCKED] stated that "Che" Guevara had gone to Bolivia in accordance wit the same "right" as that under which Guevara had come to Cuba to aid Castro in the revolutionary struggle against Batista: The "right" of every Latin American to contribute to the liberation of his country and the entire continent of Latin America. Castro then said that he wished to explain the revolutionary tradition in Latin America, and went on to describe the feats of the leading Latin American "liberators," notably Bolivar and San Martin.

5. Castro added that Cuba did not agree with the Soviet approach to "wars of national liberation" in Latin America. He accused the USSR of having turned its back upon its own revolutionary tradition and of having moved to a point where it would refuse to support any revolutionary movement unless the actions of the latter contributed to the achievement of Soviet objectives, as contrasted to international communist objectives. Castro said that in recent years the Soviet Union had not honored the principle aim of true communism, i.e., the liberation of mankind throughout the world. Castro concluded by stating that regardless of the attitudes of the Soviet Union, Cuba would support any revolutionary movement which it considered as contributing to the achievement of this objective.

6. Despite the open disagreement concerning revolutionary action, the discussions with Kosygin concerning economic and military aid from the Soviet Union to Cuba were held in an amicable atmosphere. The Soviets indicated that they were willing to continue to supply Cuba with considerable amounts of economic aid and that they military aid programs, especially those concerned with the modernization of the Cuban armed forces, would be continued.

7. After Kosygin's departure the Cuban leadership assessed the visit as having been a useful one. The Cuban leaders judged that they had clearly explained the Cuban revolutionary attitude to the Soviets, but that there had been no serious deterioration of relations between the two nations. The Cubans were especially pleased to see that although major disagreements existed in the political sector, relations in the economic and military sectors had remained on a friendly and productive basis.

Document 36 contd.

DEPARTMENT OF STATE

AIRGRAM

F760903-1872
FOR RM USE ONLY

A-128

UNCLASSIFIED OFFICIAL USE

DECLASSIFICATION DATE

TO : Department of State   PER H. Ryan OFFICE ARA

DEPT. PASS: ASUNCION, BUENOS AIRES, BRASILIA, LIMA, MONTEVIDEO, RIO DE JANEIRO, SANTIAGO, DIA, USCINCSO

FADRC FOI CASE NO. 5-B-143
OSD

FROM : Amembassy LA PAZ   DATE: October 18, 1967

SUBJECT: Official Confirmation of Death of Che Guevara

REF :

BEGIN UNCLASSIFIED: On October 16, 1967, the High Command of the Bolivian Armed Forces released the following communique, together with three annexes, on the death of Che Guevara:

"1. In accordance with information provided for national and international opinion, based on documents released by the Military High Command on October 9 and subsequently, concerning the combat that took place at La Higuera between units of the Armed Forces and the red group commanded by Ernesto "Che" Guevara, as a result of which he, among others, lost his life, the following is established:

a) Ernesto Guevara fell into the hands of our troops gravely wounded and in full use of his mental faculties. After the combat ended, he was transferred to the town of La Higuera, more or less at 8 p.m. on Sunday, October 8, where he died as a result of his wounds. His body was transferred to the city of Vallegrande at 4 p.m. on Monday, October 9, in a helicopter of the Bolivian Air Force.

b) Two medical doctors, Dr. Moises Abraham Baptista and Dr. Jose Maria Cazo, director and intern respectively of the

Enclosures:

1. Annex 1 (Death Certificate)
2. Annex 2 (Autopsy Report)
3. Annex 3 (Argentine Police Report)
4. Communique of Argentine Embassy
5. Spanish texts of above (clippings)

UNCLASSIFIED USE

POL: CWGrover, JTBeckett, REX, ADFreeman   DCM: JWFisher

POL: CWGrover

Document 37. Dept. of State Airgram, Official Confirmation of Death of Che Guevara (October 18, 1967)

Dept. of State Airgram, Official Confirmation of Death of Che Guevara from U.S. embassy in La Paz confirming Che's death, attaching his death certificate, autopsy report, Argentine police report, Communiqué of Argentine embassy and various reports.

DECLASSIFIED

F760203-1873

LA PAZ A-128

2

Knights of Malta hospital, certified the death (Annex No. 1) and recorded the autopsy ordered by the military authorities of Vallegrande (Annex No. 2).

c) With regard to the identification of the deceased and the authentication of the diary that belonged to him, the government requested the cooperation of Argentine technical organizations, which sent three experts, one handwriting specialist and two fingerprint specialists, who verified the identity of the remains and certified that the handwriting of the campaign diary, captured by our troops, coincides with that of Ernesto Guevara (Annex No. 3).

d) The campaign diary and the book of doctrine (libro de conceptuaciones) are documents that contain an account of activities, from the date of his entry (into the guerrilla area) until October 7, and (justify) the judgments that this chief of subversion, the members of the guerrilla bands, and the people, both in this country and abroad, who collaborated with them, deserved. As a consequence, they are documents exclusively for the use of the military.

2. By this means the Military High Command considers complete all information relating to the death of Che Guevara. La Paz, October 16, 1967." END UNCLASSIFIED.

BEGIN CLASSIFIED. Comment: The reports provide further documentary proof that the guerrilla chieftain, who was reportedly fatally injured in battle against the Bolivian Armed Forces on October 8, was indeed Ernesto Che Guevara. The documents do little, however, to resolve public speculation on the timing and manner of death. It will be widely noted that neither the death certificate nor the autopsy report state a time of death (the examining physicians are said to have told journalists that Guevara died a few hours before their examination late in the afternoon of October 9). Moreover, the communique also leaves unsaid the time of death, indicating simply that it occurred sometime between 8 p.m. October 8, and the transfer of the body to Vallegrande at 4 p.m. the following afternoon. This would appear to be an attempt to bridge the difference between a series of earlier divergent statements from Armed Forces sources, ranging from assertions that he died during or shortly after battle to those suggesting he survived at least twenty-four hours. Some early reports last week also indicated that Guevara was captured with minor injuries while later statements, including the attached autopsy report, affirm that he suffered multiple and serious bullet wounds.

Document 37 contd.

UNCLASSIFIED

F760003-1874

LIMITED OFFICIAL USE

LA PAZ A-128

3

We doubt that the communique will satisfactorily answer these questions and are inclined to agree with the comment by _Presencia_ columnist _Politicus_ that these discrepancies, now that the identity of the body is generally accepted, are "going to be the new focus of polemics in the coming days, especially abroad." END CLASSI-FIED.

HENDERSON

LIMITED OFFICIAL USE
UNCLASSIFIED

Document 37 contd.

F760003-1875 ~~CLASSIFIED~~ (E262A) R

Pg. 1 of Enclosure to
LA PAZ A-128

Annex No. 1 – Death Certificate

The death certificate signed October 10, 1967, by Drs. Moises
ABRAHAM Baptista and Jose MARTINEZ Cazo, Hospital Knights of
Malta, Vallegrande, Bolivia, indicates that on October 9 at
5:30 p.m., there arrived DOA an individual who military authorities said was Ernesto GUEVARA Lynch, approximately 40 years of
age, the cause of death being multiple bullet wounds in the
thorax and extremities. Preservative was applied to the body.

Annex No. 2 – Autopsy Report

The autopsy report signed October 10, 1967 by Drs. ABRAHAM
Baptista and MARTINEZ Cazo, indicates that the body recognized
as that of Ernesto Guevara was 40 years of age, white race,
approximately 1.73 meters in height, brown curly hair, heavy
curly beard and mustache, heavy eyebrows, straight nose, thin
lips, mouth open, teeth in good order with nicotine stains,
lower left pre-molar floating, light blue eyes, regular physique,
scar along almost whole left side of back. A general examination
showed the following wounds:

1. Bullet wound in left clavicular region egressing through
shoulder blade.

2. Bullet wound in right clavicular region fracturing same,
without egress.

3. Bullet wound in right side, without egress.

4. Two bullet wounds in left side, with egress through back.

5. Bullet wound in left pectoral between 9th and 10th ribs,
with egress on left side.

6. Bullet wound in lower third part of right thigh.

7. Bullet wound in lower third part of left thigh in seton.

8. Bullet wound in lower right forearm with fractured ulva.

The thorax cavity when opened showed that the first wound lightly
injured the apex of the left lung.

Document 37 contd.

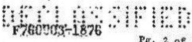

UNCLASSIFIED   Pg. 2 of Enclosure to
                                     LA PAZ A-128

The second injured the sub-clavic vessel, the bullet lodging
itself in the second vertebra.

The third transversed the right lung lodging itself in the 9th
rib.

The left lung was slightly damaged by bullet no. 4.

Wound no. 5 transversed the left lung in a tangential trajectory.

Thorax cavities, especially the right, presented abundant blood
collection.

The opened abdomen showed no traumatic lesion, only expansion
due to gases and citric liquid.

The cause of death was the thorax wounds and consequent hemorrhag-
ing.

            Annex No. 3 - Argentine Police Report

On Saturday, October 14, 1967, three officials of the Argentine
Federal Police (Investigations), one a handwriting expert and
the other two fingerprint experts, at the request of the Bolivian
Government, visited Bolivian military headquarters in La Paz to
collaborate in a matter of identification. They were shown a
metal container in which were two amputated hands in a liquid
solution, apparently formaldehyde.

The fingerprint experts tried the "Juan Vucetich" system used in
Argentina of making papillary sketches of the fingers, but the
liquid caused the fingertips to wrinkle making tracing impossible.
They then proceeded to take fingerprint impressions on polyethelene
sheets and in some cases on pieces of latex, these to be sent to
the Identification Department of the Argentine Police for further
examination.

The experts then compared the fingerprints with the copy of the
prints made from Guevara's Argentine identity record No. 3.524.272,
establishing beyond doubt that both prints were from the same
person. Also checked were prints taken from Guevara at Vallegrande
on October 9, with the same result.

The handwriting expert then examined two notebooks in good condition. The title page of one read "1967" and its reverse "Carl

                    UNCLASSIFIED

Document 37 contd.

DECLASSIFIED

F760903-1877

UNCLASSIFIED

Pg. 3 of Enclosure to
LA PAZ A-128

Klippel - Kaiserstrasca 75 - Frankfurt a.M" and "Harstellung
Baier & Schosider - Neilbreum A.N." This book shows handwriting beginning under the date of January 1, 1967 and continuing until October 7, 1967. Considering the period of the
writing, the writing itself, and the "signatures," the expert
decided they were suitable for formal extrinsic and intrinsic
comparisons in the handwriting identification system. The
expert also examined statistically the handwriting characteristics of the notebook enscribed "Elba 66509" containing 44
pages of handwriting. There was sufficient regularity of
characteristics to determine that they were the same as those
reproduced in Guevara's Argentine identity record. Copies of the material will
be forwarded to the Argentine Police for further study.

Signed by Esteban Belzhauser and Juan Carlos Delgado.

Enclosure No. 4

COMMUNIQUE OF THE ARGENTINE EMBASSY AT LA PAZ

The technical commission detailed by the Argentine Government at the request of the Bolivian Government to prove the
identity of the remains of Ernesto Guevara has proceeded to make
a comparison of the items that were provided by the Commander in
Chief of the Armed Forces with those that were in the hands of
Argentine police authorities. From the fingerprint and handwriting skill practiced by the technicians, in accordance with
scientific procedures currently in use, it develops that the
items compared correspond in an irrefutable manner to Ernesto
Guevara, thereby agreeing with the report issued by the Bolivian
authorites.

La Paz, October 16, 1967.

UNCLASSIFIED

Document 37 contd.

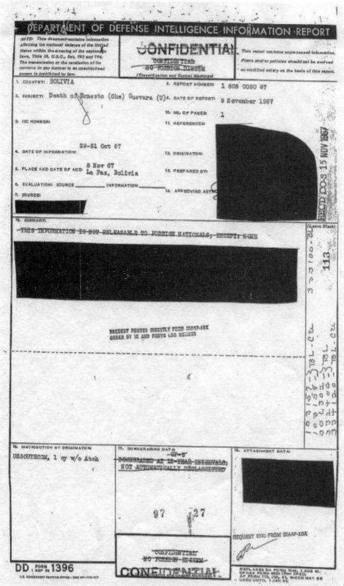

Document 38. Dept. of Defense Intelligence Information Report debriefing key Bolivian troops involved in capture and murder of Che (November 9, 1967)
    Dept. of Defense Intelligence Information Report setting forth debriefing from October 29-31, 1967 of the key Bolivian troops involved in capture and murder of Che. It purports to be an early explanation of "the important conflicts of the Valle Grande and Higueras operational areas." It also gives one version of Che's last requests and his murder.

As all of these notes were taken without the aid of a diary or available maps, it is expected that certain descrepancies will arise in regards to exact times and locations. This history is designed as only an early orientation toward the important conflicts of the Valle Grande and Higueras operational areas.

Document 38 contd.

CONFIDENTIAL

NO FOREIGN DISSEM

During the period 29 October to 31 October, ██████████ of █ Company,
██ Ranger Bn██ ██████ of █ Platoon, █ Company, ██████ of █ Platoon,
█ Company██ and one unnamed officer of █ Company commented on different aspects
of the activities of the Ranger Bn during the period 26 September to 14 October.
The following is a compilation of their remarks. The majority of the text was
solicited from ████████████████████████████████████
██████████████████, excepting that portion dealing with the demise of Che Guevara.

Resulting from information received after the battle at Higueras on the
26th of September(where Coco Parado was killed), the Ranger Bn was given the
mission of setting up a screening force along the river San Antonio to prevent
exfiltration of the G force from the area of operations. The Bn left Esperanza
at 1600 on the 26th and arrived at Pucara at 1100 hrs on the 27th. From Pucara,
Company █ and Company █ proceeded to Valle Grande while Company █ and one section
of mortars(2) moved to Chañarol by way of Quiñal and San Antonio. During the
movement to Chañarol, ████████ received information that there was G activity
around the town of San Antonio. Company █, minus the mortar section, moved from
the town into the Quebrada(ravine) San Antonio. During the approach, the company
observed through binocular one G cutting through the brush. They assumed that
this man was acting as point for a larger force, and deployed to form an ambush.
At this time, one mortar was brought up to support the operation. ████████
platoons formed an L shaped ambush to act as the blocking force while █ platoon
initiated pursuit. █ Platoon moved up the quebrada toward the blocking force and
drove the G into the area of the █ platoon, where he was captured.(see diagram 2)
The G was known as "Camba", and appeared to be in poor health and was poorly clothed.

CONFIDENTIAL NO FOREIGN DISSEM

Document 38 contd.

~~CONFIDENTIAL~~

2   ~~NO FOREIGN DISSEM~~

He stated that he had been separated from the rest of the force since the battle at La Higueras, and was traveling in this area in hopes of contacting Ramon(Che Guevara).

The capture of "Gamba" had an immediate moral effect on the troops. Previously they had thought of the Gs as very strong and clever, but after seeing "Gamba" without shoes and suffering from malnutrition, they gained confidence in their ability to destroy the G band. The soldiers began to joke and deride "Gamba" asking him why he hadn't stayed at home. "Gamba" apparently was very contrite, and this also sparked confidence and courage among the troops.

The company moved on to Charñol, where they rested for the remainder of the day. On the 28th, ███████ began sending out patrols and intelligence teams, dressed in civilian clothes. One team brought back information that a house nearby had been a possible refuge for one or two Gs. This was not fully investigated until the Company received word that "Leon" had been captured by Company ██ on 1 August, after they had moved south from Valle Grande. Company ██ sent word to ██████ that "Leon" was supposed to have stayed at a house in Charñol for a few days. The intell. team returned to the house, and after a thorough search, discovered a carbine and severa hundred rounds of ammunition. As Charñol is one of the only fording sites for the Rio Grande in the area, it appeared that the G force had been planning to move through this area an exfiltrate. However, the arrival of the 8n. in this region, plus the additional support of Company ████ and one company of ██ at Charñol, probably caused the G leaders to attempt another xit farther west. This, or the extrem asthmatic problems of Guevara, caused the G force to move to higher ground in the La Higueras area.

On 2 October, ██ platoon, ██ platoon, and one mortar section of Company ██ departed

~~CONFIDENTIAL   NO FOREIGN DISSEM~~

Document 38 contd.

CONFIDENTIAL   NO FORLIGH DISSEM

17 Gs in the Quebrada de Churro. As ███ did not have mortars, he communicated to
███████ the information and asked for support. ███████ sent the █ Platoon
and 2 mortars to Higueras to support Lt Perez. ████████████

The combined units of Company █ and the supporting units from Company █ moved
into the area of the Quebrada Churro using two squads of Company █ as a blocking force
a few KMs north of the small Quebrada Gaino. ███████ set up his mortar section
east of the Quebrada Churro, with █ Platoon of █ company to his rear in support,
under the command of ███████. █ Platoon of █ company under the command of ███████
entered the Quebrada Churro to the north and the confluence of two small streams.
███████ initiated the pursuit and began driving the G force south while ███
███ mortars shelled the ravine. At this point a machine gun was brought up to also
cover the ravine and hold the left flank of ███████ mortar section and supporting
troops.(see diagram 3) As the █ Platoon of █ company pushed south they came under
fire and lost 3 soldiers immediately. ████████ then ordered ███████ to move
down the small quebrada Tuscal and wait at the entrance of the Quebrada Churro. The
█ Platoon of █ company carried out this order and after finding nothing, was
ordered to enter the Quebrada Churro and begin pursuit in the direction of ███████
platoon. ████████ immediately encountered a group of 6 to 8 Gs and opened fire. At
this point they killed "Antonio" and "Orturo", two Cubans. ███████ lost one
soldier here and received another wounded. Apparently this action broke up the
bank and Ramon(Guevara) and "Willy" tried to break out in the direction of the
mortar section. They were sighted by the machine gun crew which took them under
fire. "Ramon"(Guevara) was hit in the lower calf and was helped by "Willy" toward the
Quebrada Tuscal, where apparently they rested for a few minutes. They then moved
north, directly in front of ███████ who ordered several soldiers to chase them.
████████████ were the first Bolivians to lay hands on Guevara.
"Willy" and "Ramon"(Guevara) were later transported back to La Higueras with ███

CONFIDENTIAL

Document 38 contd.

CONFIDENTIAL NO FOREIGN DISSEM

███ and the elements of ██ and ██ Companies. The Bolivians did not remain in position after nightfall. From 1900 hrs until 0400 hrs on the 9th, there were no significant Bolivian troops in the area of the fire-fight. This gave the G force ample time to escape the area, but either due to confusion after the battle or poor evaluation of the situation by their leaders, the G force remained in the Quebrada Churro.

On 30 October 67, at a small Kiosco in La Esperanza Bolivia, ██████ ████████████████████████████, stated the following in regards to the handling of Ernesto "Che" Guevara. Guevara and Willy were transported back to La Higueres on the afternoon of the 8th, after the battle at the Quebrada Churro. Guevara had a slight wound in the lower calf, which was treated upon returning to Higueras. ██████ talked at length with Guevara, though Guevara did not reveal any pertinent information. ██████ felt a high regard for Guevara as a soldier and man, and was anxious to know more of this "legendary figure". Guevara answered all of his questions with remarks such as "perhaps" or "possibly". Early in the morning of the 9th of October, the unit received the order to execute Guevara and the other captives. Previously, ████████████████ ████, had given express orders to keep the prisoners alive. The Officers involved did not know where the order originated, but felt that it came from the highest echelons. ██████ gave the order to execute Guevara to ████████ but he was unable to carry out the order and in turn gave it to ██████████. At this time ██████ asked Guevara if there was anything he wished before his execution. Guevara replied that he only wished to "die with a full stomach." ██████ then asked him if he was a "materialist", by having requested only food. Guevara returned to his previous tranquil manner and answered only "perhaps"

CONFIDENTIAL

NO FOREIGN DISSEM

Document 38 contd.

6   CONFIDENTIAL NO FOREIGN DISSEM

██████ then called him a "poor shit" and left the room. By this time,

████████ had fortified his courage with several beers and returned to

the room where Guevara was being held prisoner. When ██████ entered the room,

Guevara stood up, hands tied in front, and stated, "I know what you have come

for—I am ready." ██████ looked at him for a few minutes and then said, "No

you are mistaken—be seated." ██████ then left the room for a few moments.

"Willy", the prisoner taken with Guevara, was being held in a small house

a few meters away. While ██████ was waiting outside to get his nerve back,

████████ entered and shot "Willy". "Willy" was a Cuban and according to

the sources had been an instigator of the riots among the miners in Bolivia.

Guevara heard the burst of fire in his room and for the first time appeared

to be frightened. ████████ returned to the room where Guevara was being

held. When he entered, Guevara stood and faced the ████████████ told

him to be seated but he refused to sit down and stated, "I will remain standing

for this." The ██ began to get angry and told him to be seated again, but

Guevara would say nothing. Finally Guevara told him, "Know this now, you are

killing a man." ██████ then fired a burst from his M2 Carbine, knocking Guevarra back

into the wall of the small house.

Interviews with a doctor that had examined Guevara's cadaver and evaluation of

available photos indicate that Guevara did have one wound in the lower calf,

that appeared to the Doctor to have been received at a different time then the

other wounds that were received at short range and directly from the front.

During the evening of the 8th and the morning of the 9th, ████████ had

on his person a pipe that he said Gueva a had given him during their night

together at La Higuera. He showed this pipe to ████████ and ████████

CONFIDENTIAL NO FOREIGN DISSEM

Document 38 contd.

7

The pipe was of an "air cooling design" with a part of the stem exposed and made of silver colored metal. The bowl was black and appeared to have been smoked for some time. This pipe form agrees with the descriptions of the pipe "Ramon" had been using during earlier developments of the G operations.

At 0400 hrs on the morning of the 9th, Elements of ▪ and ▪ company returned to the Quebrad Churro and reengaged the G force. ▪▪ Platoon of Company ▪ and a mortar squad formed the blocking force and the confluence of the Quebrada and ▪▪▪▪▪ platoon of ▪ company began pursuit towards them. (▪▪▪▪▪ was with the mortars at this time and could observe the movement of the Gs in the Quebrada. He took 6 men and entered the Quebrada and shot "El Chino" and Lorgio Voca. These were the only two Gs who fell in this action. After the initial contact, the Gs could not be located so ▪▪▪▪ initiated patrols throughout the area. At nightfall the units again returned to EA Higueras, leaving the area open.

The two companies patrolled the area from 10-12 October trying to regain contact. On the 12th intelligence was received that the G force had broken into two small groups trying to move out of the area through Portero. Company ▪ departed La Higueras and headed in the direction of Portero, by Picacho and Tranco Mayo. At Trancho Mayo they could observe the ▪▪▪ Gs with two young guides moving toward Portero. They could not determine exactly how many were in the group. To arrive ahead of the Gs who were moving along a Quebrada, The Company used the road and were able to get into position at Portero twenty

Document 38 contd.

8   **T.C FOREIGN DISSEM** ~~CONFIDENTIAL~~

minutes before they sighted the Gs moving up the Quebrada in their direction.
████████ with a squad and one mortar formed a blocking force at the mouth
of the Quebrada. ██ Platoon of ██ company entered the Quebrada behind the Gs
and initiated pursuit. When ████████ and his men opened fire on the Gs they
began to leap about. This confused ████████ soldiers though they continued
to fire. The Gs doubled back and climbed out of the Quebrada before the ██
Platoon could bring them under fire. ██ Platoon pursued them up the hill but
lost contact at the top.

No casualties were suffered in this engagement and no Gs fell, though they
did drop their rucksacks when brought under fire by ████████. The rucksacks
contained food, various documents, and drugs. Surgical tools were also among
the equipment in the rucksacks. ████████ was unable to describe the documents
or the origin of the medical supplies.

On 13 August the Company attempted to block the Gs again East of Portero but
the Gs immediately attacked one point of the circle and were able to break out
killing 2 soldiers. By noon of the 13th the Company had lost contact completely
with the G force.

The second group was contacted by ██ Company on 14 October at El Cajon. This
fight resulting in the death of 4 Gs. El Chapaco, a bolivian, El Saldado, a
bolivian, an unnamed Bolivian, and one unnamed Cuban. This fight on the 14th
was the last contact made b the Ranger Bn before leaving the area of operationns.
None of the ████████████████ had details on this fight or could
draw a map as to the exact location of El Cajon.   ~~CONFIDENTIAL~~

The original G force was 17. 7 were killed in action by Companies ██ and
██ and 4 were destroyed by ██ Company at El Cajon. Recent reports indicate that
the Cubans have disarmed the Bolivian Gs and seem to have them under guard.
Apparently there is some sort of disagreement in the operation within the G

9

organization. One farmer informed the authorities that the Gs ate at his farm and rested. During this time, the Bolivians were kept separate from the Cubans and were watched closely by the Cubans. The Bolivians had no arms. All of the Gs are shaved and have their hair cut. Officials believe that they are trying to move out of the area through Abapo or Cabezas.

Document 38 contd.

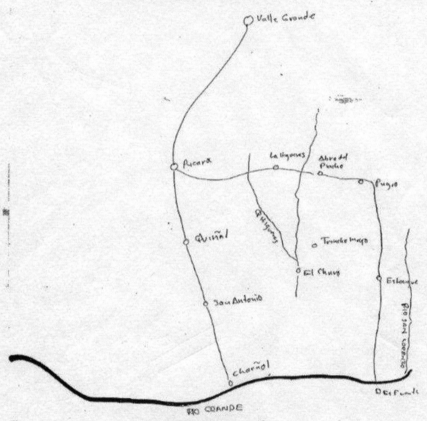

CONFIDENTIAL

NC FOREIGN DISSEM

Document 39. Hand-drawn maps from the debriefing of the Bolivian troops of the last battles with the guerillas and attempts to capture Harry Villegas (Pombo) (November 9, 1967)

Hand-drawn maps from the debriefing of the Bolivian troops of the last battles with the guerillas and the attempts to capture Harry Villegas (Pombo) and his comrades.

DIAGRAM 2
CAPTURE OF "GAMBA"

CONFIDENTIAL
~~NO FOREIGN DISSEM~~

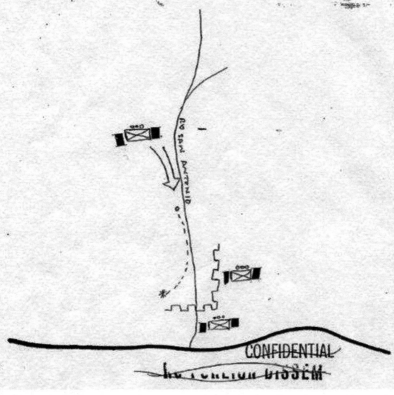

CONFIDENTIAL
~~NO FOREIGN DISSEM~~

Document 39 contd.

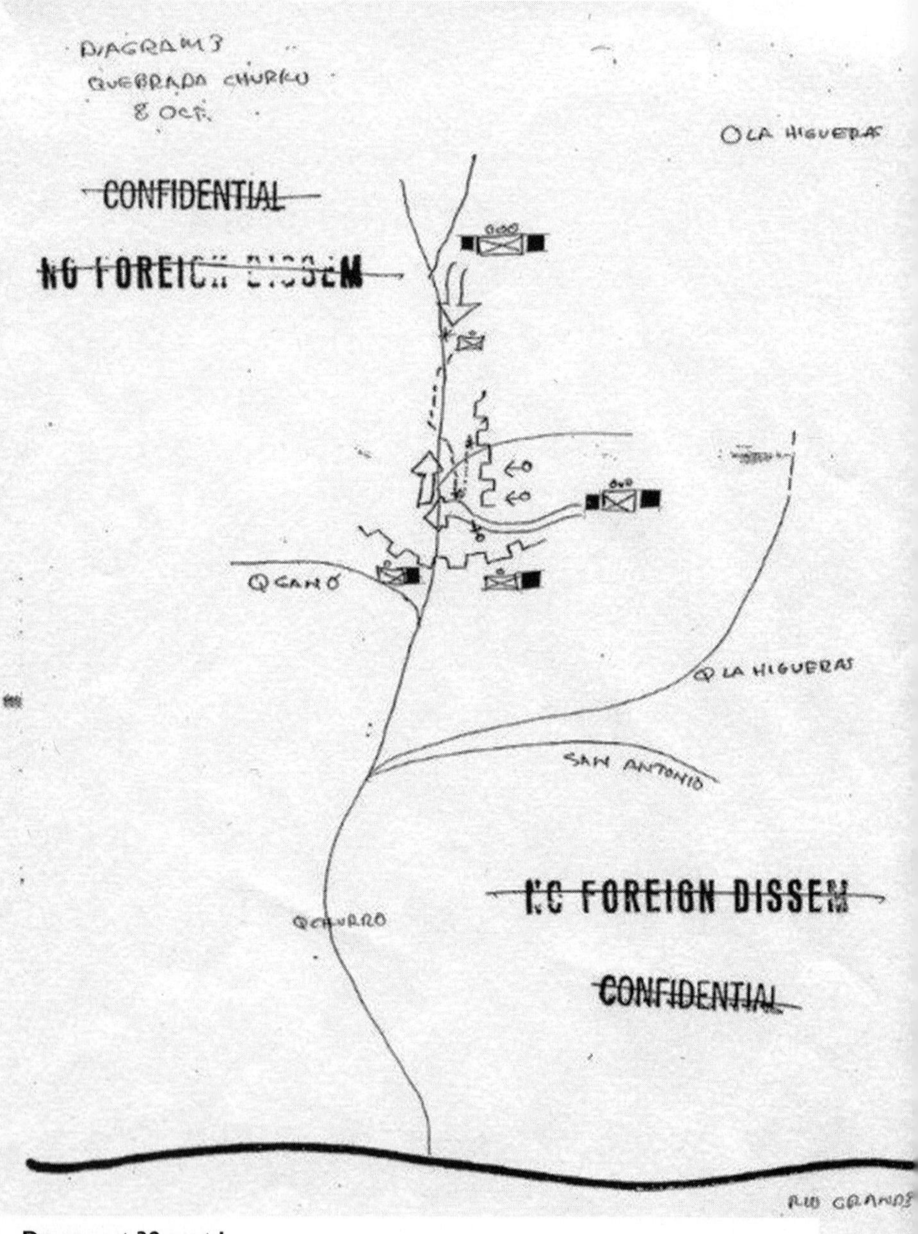

DIAGRAM 3
QUEBRADA CHURRO
8 OCT.

O LA HIGUERAS

CONFIDENTIAL

NO FOREIGN DISSEM

Q CANO

Q LA HIGUERAS

SAN ANTONIO

NO FOREIGN DISSEM

CONFIDENTIAL

Q CHURRO

RIO GRANDE

Document 39 contd.

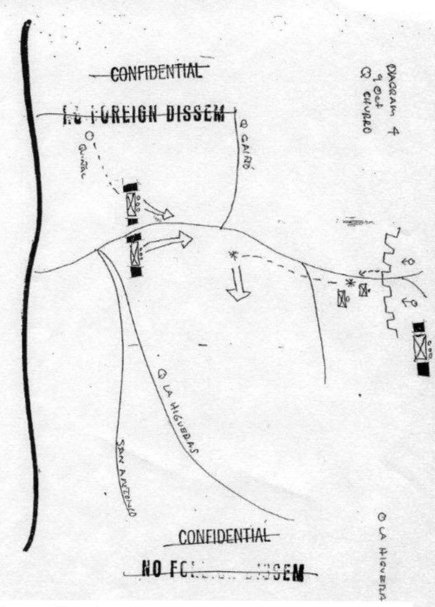

Document 39 contd.

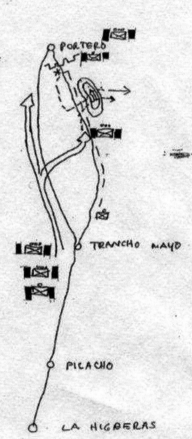

DIAGRAM 5
PURSUIT OF "POMBO"

~~CONFIDENTIAL~~

~~NO FOREIGN DISSEM~~

PORTERO

TRANCHO MAYO

PICACHO

LA HIGBERAS

~~CONFIDENTIAL~~

~~NO FOREIGN DISSEM~~

Document 39 contd.

SECRET

INSPECTOR GENERAL
75-20

3 June 1975

MEMORANDUM FOR: Deputy Inspector General

SUBJECT: Statement by [_____] concerning
his assignment Bolivia in 1967 and his role
in the capture of Ernesto "Che" GUEVARA
de la Serna

REFERENCE: Memo dated 29 May 1975

1. The undersigned met with [_____] contract
employee, on 2 and 3 June to obtain his story about his
assignment to Bolivia in 1967. This query is based upon ref
interview, during which [_____] mentioned that he had re-
transmitted an order from Colonel [_____]
Commander of the 8th Division of the Bolivian Army, to a
Bolivian sergeant, which resulted in the execution of Ernesto
"Che" GUEVARA de la Serna, Cuban leader of the guerrillas then
operating in Bolivia.

2. [_____] said that his assignment came about after an
interview held in Miami in June or July of 1967, at which time
he was a case officer working for the Miami office. He had
been selected for the job interview because of his paramilitary training and experience. He was asked if he would
agree to serve with [_____] a fellow Cuban. He
accepted. He was told that he was to go to Bolivia with
[_____] where they would be engaged in training intelligence
teams for the 2nd Ranger Battalion of the Eighth Division of
the Bolivian Army. He was also told that he and [_____]
would be assigned to the 2nd Ranger Battalion as advisors
and would be based in the town of Esperanza. While in Miami,
he and [_____] were given briefings about the political and
guerrilla situation in Bolivia, and he was given a refresher
course in communications. [_____] and [_____] were told
that there were strong indications that Guevara was leading
the guerrillas. Among the instructions given them was a clear
one that in the event that the Bolivian Army captured Guevara,
they should do everything possible "to keep him alive."

3. They were introduced to their future case officer
in Washington, who was to be in liaison with the Bolivian
forces in Santa Cruz.

Document 40. CIA debriefing of Felix Rodriguez (June 3, 1975)
This CIA debriefing (June 3, 1975) of Felix Rodriguez was prepared almost eight
years after Che's death for the CIA's Deputy Inspector General. He was investigating
assassinations by the CIA for the Church Committee of the Senate. There was an obvious
interest in covering the CIA's role and giving President Johnson plausible deniability. It
was approved for release in 1993 under the CIA Historical Review program.

4. Prior to their departure, both [...] and [   ]
were issued false U.S. re-entry permits in the names of
[   ] and [-   ] respectively. . These were
received in New York City just prior to their departure on
30 July for La Paz on a Braniff Airline flight. Their case
officer had preceded them and met them on 31 July at 7 a.m.
at the La Paz airport. [........] believes that Bolivian visas
were stamped in their re-entry permits. .

5. The case officer and another American took them to
meet [   ] to whom they were introduced as
experts on guerrilla warfare. He issued each a personal card
in which were handwritten his instructions to all civilian
and military officials that they be given full support. At
ten that morning, they met [   ] Commander-in-Chief
of the Bolivian Armed Forces. (It wasn't until about a month
later that [   ] met [   ] in Santa Cruz.) While in
La Paz, no new instructions were issued to them about their
mission. After about a week there, they were flown to Santa
Cruz de la Sierra for a few days and introduced to Colonel
[   ] Commander of the Eighth Division.
[   ] arranged for [... .   ] the American
officer in charge of the military mission training the 2nd
Ranger Battalion, to come to Santa Cruz to meet [   ] and
[   ] They were also introduced to Major [   ]
G-2 of the Eighth Division. After 3 or 4 days in Santa Cruz,
[   ] and [.] went to La Esperanza, where they were
quartered at the Bolivian officers' compound. In La Esperanza
they met [   ] the Commander of the 2nd Ranger Battalion,
and Captain [. ...)

6. Prior to their departure from La Paz, [..] and
[...] were issued Bolivian uniforms and credentials as
captains in the Bolivian Army. Nevertheless, they did not
receive Bolivian Army insignia. Later, [   ] was given by
[. . ...] a Bolivian tri-color cap-insignia which he wore
(escarapela). [   ] and [...] were issued Smith and Wesson
double-action automatic pistols. During their activities as instructors and advisors they assumed the role of Bolivian
officers, although they were known as foreign advisors to a
number of Bolivian officers. [   ] said that he learned later
that the American Ambassador had prohibited anyone other than
he and [......] from becoming involved in the anti-guerrilla
activities in the field.)

7. Despite their apparent status as Bolivian officers,
[   ] said that they never were given orders by higher-
ranking Bolivian officers (One exception to this rule was the
order which Colonel [...] issued to [   ] on the day of
Guevara's execution, if [.] story is to be believed.)

-3-

8. [   ] was assigned to Santa Cruz and [   ] was assigned to La Esperanza, where the latter conducted most of the intelligence training. As time went by, [   ] own duties gravitated to becoming basically those of an advisor. He said that his case officer was aware of and approved of this development. Among the things which [   ] s[and [   ] attempted to accomplish was the preservation of the lives of captured guerrillas, for the collection of intelligence about the guerrilla's locations, as well as for humanitarian reasons. [   ], said that he saved the life of Jose Castillo Chavez, traveling for that purpose to Vallegrande from Santa Cruz, where he spoke briefly to Castillo at the Nuestra Senora de Malta Hospital. At this time [   ] learned of the intent of [   ] of the Rangers. to have the prisoner executed. [   ] prevailed on Major [   ] and [   ] to take his side. The prisoner was flown to Vallegrande where [   ] covered all medical costs and carried out a two-week interrogation. The resulting twenty-page interrogation report provided the Bolivians with a complete concept of the guerrilla's strategy, which turned out to be the key to Guevara's capture, according to [.] This report was attributed by the Bolivians to be from their own people.

9. This important development was followed by an encounter in late September between a unit led by a Lt. [   ] and the remnants of the guerrillas. During this action, a Cuban lieutenant named Miguel; the Bolivian Coco Peredo; and a Bolivian physician named Jose Gutierrez Ardaya were killed. [   ] travelled by jeep to Pucara, where the bodies were located, and through the information he had learned from Castillo, he was able to establish that the men were from Guevara's forward element. Upon his return to Santa Cruz, [   ] advised [   ] that the 2nd Ranger Battallion should be immediately deployed, with the remaining two weeks of their training cancelled. [   ] accepted this advice and the Rangers were moved to Pucara, and the Headquarters of the Eighth Division were moved to Vallegrande. [   ] continued in his advisory role, suggesting areas for troop deployment as well as the deployment of the intelligence teams. On the 8th of October, contact was established with Guevara's remaining forces. (At this time [   ] was in Vallegrande and [   ] in Esperanza.) On the 8th, Major [   ] reported over the radio that "the chief" had been captured. [   ] then flew over the area in a PT-6 carrying with him a PRC-10 radio with which he was able to communicate with the Bolivian forces. He then confirmed that Guevara was "the chief" who had been captured. He returned to Vallegrande where he told [   ] that Guevara had been wounded and captured.

Document 40 contd.

-4-

10. That day [   ] was sent to Higueras to interrogate the guerrilla prisoners and assembled the captured documents. Since Colonel, [   ] was planning to fly by helicopter to Higueras on the 9th, [   ] asked him on the evening of the 8th if he could accompany him to interrogate Guevara. [   ] consulted his staff and agreed. (The helicopter had room only for a pilot and two passengers.) [   ] prepared a 100-word message to the [---] in code reporting Guevara's capture and asking that an Embassy representative be sent to the area to prevail upon the Bolivians to spare Guevara's life, since he did not believe that he could succeed in doing so. This message was prepared for the scheduled 10 a.m. transmission of 9 October, and was not transmitted to the relay point in Asuncion, Paraguay, until about 10:30 a.m., after [   ] arrived in Higueras and set up his radio transmitter an RS-48.

11. [   ] [   ] and the pilot, [   ] set out by helicopter from Vallegrande at 7:15 a.m. on the 9th, and arrived in Higueras at about 7:40 a.m. [   ] accompanied [   ] and Major [   ] when they visited Guevara in the school room which was his improvised jail. Guevara would not answer [   ] when spoken to. He was bound, hand and foot, and had a leg wound.

12. [   ] and Major [   ] then reviewed the captured documents and [   ] s] obtained permission from [   ] to photograph all the papers, including Guevara's diary, and also [   ] s] permission to retain the original accommodation addresses found.

13. While [   ] and all the other Bolivian officers (with the exception of a Lieutenant [   ] were outside of the village attending to other military affairs, [...] remained in Higueras as the highest ranking "Bolivian officer". In this capacity he answered a call received on the military field telephone and answered as Captain [   ] He was given the code numbers 500 and 600 as orders which were to be implemented by command of "higher authorities". He said that the connection was not clear and he could not recognize the voice but it could have been that of Major [   ] In any case, [   ] said that since it was a line only available to the military he was confident that it was order re-transmitted through military channels. He said that he knew that 500 referred to Guevara, 600 to the word execute and 700 to the preservation of Guevara's life. These simple codes had been identified to him previously.

Document 40 contd.

-5-

14. Upon [   ] return, [/\ ] told him of the
message and [   ] took it as an authentic order and made
no effort to have it confirmed. [/\ ] asked if Guevara's
life could be preserved since he had these instructions.
[   ] replied that his own position would be placed in
jeopardy if he did not comply. [/\ ] asked him to make
the attempt anyway. [/\ ] believes that [   ] had
already resigned himself to the inevitability of Guevara's
execution.) [   ] said that he was in sympathy with
wish but that it was not in his power to reverse the order.
He told [/\ ] that he was well aware of the treatment which
Fidel had meted out to Cubans and told him to execute Guevara
in any manner which he might choose. [   ] said that he
had to leave for Vallegrande at 10:00 a.m. and would send
a helicopter back to pick up Guevara's "body" at 2 p.m., and
"as a friend", asked that the body be ready.
reiterated his request that the order be appealed and
agreed to make the attempt, and said he would advise if he
were successful.

15. Failing a counter-manding of the order and as the
senior "Bolivian officer" left in Higueras, [   ] said he
was left with the implementation of the execution. After
[   ] left, [   ] was able to talk to Guevara, who
identified [/\ ] either as a Puerto Rican or a Cuban
working for U.S. intelligence. He said he made this judgment
on the basis of the questions asked and on [/\ ] accent.
While [/\ ] was with Guevara, shots were fired in adjoining
rooms and [/\ ] later determined that these involved the
execution of two other prisoners. Recognizing these shots
for what they were, nevertheless, Guevara blanched when
[/\ ] confirmed that he too would be executed; although
later composing himself.

16. After leaving Guevara, [/\ ] told a sergeant of
the order to execute Guevara and entrusted the mission to him.
He was told to fire below the head. The order was given to
the sergeant at 1:00 p.m. and [/\ ] heard the shots fired
at Guevara at 1:20 p.m. At 2:00 p.m., the helicopter returned
to Higueras. A Father [   ] performed the last rites and
Guevara's remains were strapped to one of the helicopter's
skids and [   ] accompanied them to Vallegrande, where
they landed at 2:30 p.m. [   ] said that he lost himself
quickly in the crowd gathered at the airport, but that
[   ] took charge of the remains and was photographed.
[   ] said that the title of the photograph, which appeared
in the press, gave an incorrect identification of
the name [   ] used, [   ]

Document 40 contd.

-6-

17. [   ] said he reported the executions to Major
[   ] and the Chief of Operations, a [
and then was taken back to identify the bodies of the three
executed guerrillas. They then drove to Santa Cruz with the
documents, films and equipment and then flew to La Paz,
where [   ] contacted his case officer. He was taken to
a home where the [   ] and other Americans were briefed by
him. Everything which he had been able to retain was turned
in then to be carried by a special courier to Washington.
[   ] then flew back to Santa Cruz where a C-130 ordered
by General Porter, CINCSOUTH, was to pick him and [   ]
up for a flight to the Canal Zone. This plane arrived with
a flat tire on the 10th or 11th. The U.S. Mission aircraft,
a C-54, was then flown to Santa Cruz and he and [
were flown back to La Paz. After overnighting there, another
C-130 carried them to Panama where [   ] was asked to
relate his story to General Porter. After 2 weeks in Panama,
[   ] and [   ] were documented as GS-16s so that they
could board a over-booked military flight to Charlotte,
South Carolina. After their arrival there, they journeyed
to Miami, where [   ] briefed General Cushman. [
believes that in both high-level briefings he mentioned his
own personal role in the execution of Guevara.)

Document 40 contd.

C   ƒ   ~~Secret~~   S

DIRECTORATE OF
INTELLIGENCE

The Che Guevara Diary

Special Report
WEEKLY REVIEW

~~Secret~~

№   3

15 December 1967
SC No. 00600/67A

Document 41. CIA Director of Intelligence analysis of *The Guevara Diary*, Cuban Attempts to Export Revolution (Dec. 15, 1967)
This CIA analysis of Che's *Diary* concludes that "when the diary is published the Guevara legend will only be dulled by this account of the pathetic struggle in Bolivia."

Secret

Special Reports are supplements to the Current Intelligence Weeklies issued by the Office of Current Intelligence. The Special Reports are published separately to permit more comprehensive treatment of a subject. They are prepared by the Office of Current Intelligence, the Office of Research and Reports, or the Directorate of Science and Technology. Special Reports are coordinated as appropriate among the Directorates of CIA, but, except for the normal substantive exchange with other agencies at the working level, have not been coordinated outside CIA unless specifically indicated.

WARNING

This document contains information affecting the national defense of the United States, within the meaning of Title 18, sections 793 and 794, of the US Code, as amended. Its transmission or revelation of its contents to or receipt by an unauthorized person is prohibited by law.

DISSEMINATION CONTROLS

This document MUST NOT BE RELEASED TO FOREIGN GOVERN-MENTS. If marked with specific dissemination controls in accordance with the provisions of DCID 1/7, the document must be handled within the framework of the limitation so imposed.

Document 41 contd.

THE CHÉ GUEVARA DIARY

The diary of Ernesto "Che" Guevara is the protracted memoirs of the ill-fated guerrilla movement he led in the Bolivian backlands from 7 November 1966 to 8 October 1967. The account, which was found with Guevara after his capture, reveals that the guerrilla band suffered from the outset from dissension and ineptitude that compounded the hardships of jungle operations. Guevara's movement ultimately failed because the Bolivian peasants received the guerrillas with fear and suspicion.

Guevara, in his diary, wrote simply, without metaphor or embellishing prose. He did not discuss ideological or substantive political matters and avoided personal ruminations and reminiscences. He said virtually nothing that can be turned into inspiring mottoes or myths. It seems, moreover, that when the diary is published the Guevara legend will only be dulled by this account of the pathetic struggle in Bolivia.

Cuban Attempt to Export Revolution

The diary shows that Guevara's 11-month odyssey was a concerted attempt by Cuba to open the central heartland of South America to international guerrilla insurgency. Since the first Tri-Continent Conference in Havana in January 1966, Fidel Castro had been insisting that "it is the duty of every revolutionary to make revolution." Jules Regis Debray in his *Revolution Within Revolution* charted the ideological fiber of Castro's militant stand, and it was left to Guevara, presumed revolutionary consummate, to lead the "inevitable struggle."

It is clear from the diary that the guerrillas were carefully selected and trained, and were well equipped by Cuba. At least three members of the central committee of the Cuban Communist Party, and perhaps a dozen or so other Cubans—all followers of Guevara and experts in guerrilla tactics—were with the band. In short, Castro and Guevara set out systematically to prove Debray's corollary to militant Castroism: that the Latin American guerrilla movement ought to be an internationalized rural insurgency springing from the rebellion of a frustrated and oppressed peasantry.

Guevara's hopeless struggle and demise, however, proved only

Page 1   SPECIAL REPORT   15 Dec 67

Document 41 contd.

BOLIVIA: Area of Guevara's Guerrilla Activity

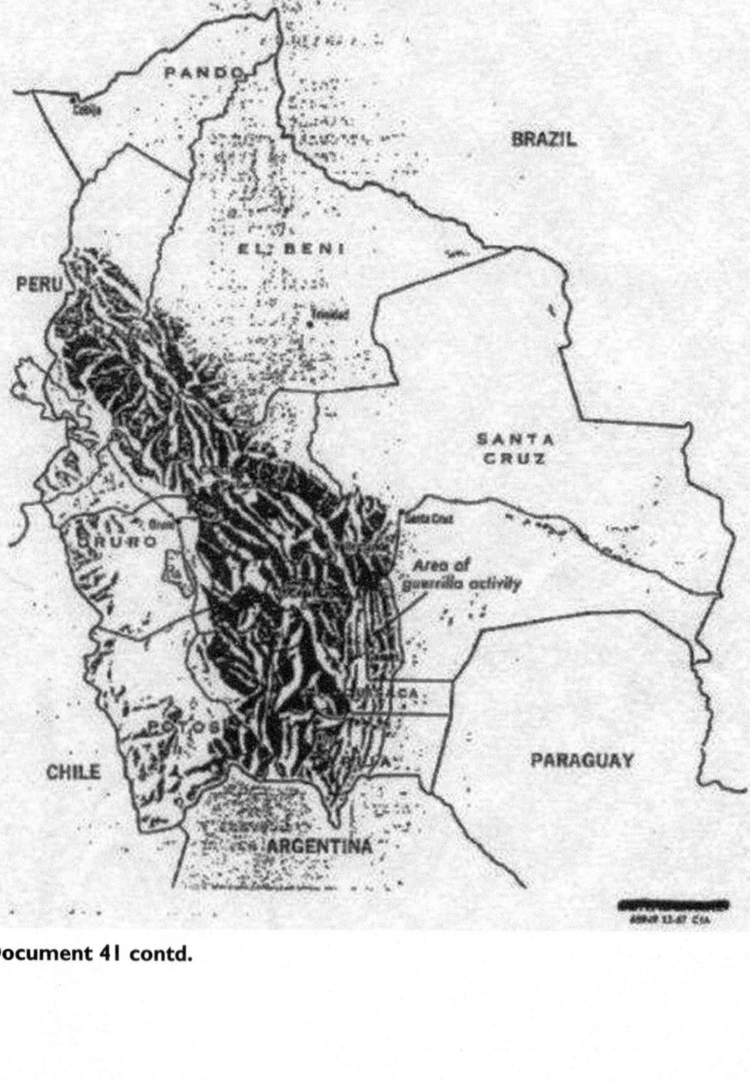

PANDO

BRAZIL

PERU

EL BENI

Trinidad

SANTA
CRUZ

ORURO

Santa Cruz

Area of
guerrilla activity

POTOSI

CHILE

PARAGUAY

ARGENTINA

Document 41 contd.

the futility of the approach. The
Debray strategy and the guerrilla
tactics that Che compiled in his
handbook *Guerrilla Warfare* proved
to be empty theoretics. Guevara
was unable to win the support of
the Bolivian Communist Party
(PCB-S) and could not prevent his
own group from splitting into
conflicting factions. The peasant
support considered essential to
the revolutionary thesis was entirely lacking. It was, in fact,
the hostility and suspicion of
the Bolivian peasants that forced
the band to continue its endless
flight through the jungles. Finally, after some months of inef-
fective counterguerrilla activity
by Bolivian Army units, the Bolivian Rangers were assigned to
the operation. The Rangers, well
trained in pursuit and harassment,
eventually destroyed most of the
guerrillas.

Failure of the Guerrilla Tactics

A disciplined, loyal, and
tightly organized revolutionary
cadre is the first requirement
in the Castro-Guevara-Debray blue-
print for insurgency. In *Guerrilla Warfare*, Guevara said that
"homogeneity, respect for the
leader, bravery, and familiarity
with the terrain" are the essential characteristics of the guerrilla band. In Bolivia, however,
most of these basic concepts were
violated or ignored. The band
was composed of Cuban, Bolivian,
and Peruvian nationals, none of
whom was very familiar with the
operational zone.

Guevara vainly attempted to
remedy these deficiencies. Ac-

cording to the diary, he spent
the first three months securing
bases of operations and training
and indoctrinating the guerrillas.
His first attempt at an explor-
atory familiarization trek through
the jungles, however, was plagued
by inaccurate maps and the group
became discouraged and weakened
by heavy rains, insects, and a
shortage of food and water. Ten-
sions between the Bolivians and
Cubans became serious in the first
months, and the initial explor-
atory patrols were characterized
by ineptitude, flagging morale,
and poor leadership.

Ineptitude

Communications with Havana
and La Paz were lost as early as
January when a transmitter rusted
because it was stored in a damp
cave. On 26 February, the band
suffered its first personnel loss
when a member drowned attempting
to cross a turbulent stream. On
17 March, a second member was lost
in a similar accident. Thus,
neither of Che's initial objectives—training and exploration—
was completed, and various acci-
dents had already taken their toll.

On 23 March, the guerrillas
ambushed a Bolivian patrol and
killed eight of its members. A
second battle on 10 April accounted
for seven army dead and also for
the first Cuban loss. Capt. Jesus
Suarez Gayol, a former vice minister
of the Ministry of Sugar Industries,
was killed. Guevara was discouraged
with the results of these skirmishes, which showed that the guerrillas were still divided and insufficiently trained.

Document 41 contd.

Morale

Che was particularly disturbed with the reluctance of the Bolivians to work with the Cubans, and on 12 April reminded them that "the first blood drawn was Cuban." On 25 April, Capt. Eliseo Reyes Rodriguez (San Luis), a member of the central committee of the Cuban Communist Party, was killed in combat. The loss of San Luis was a major psychological blow to Guevara, who for the first time was unabashedly despondent. He mourned that San Luis was "the best man in the guerrilla band" and a comrade "since (San Luis was) practically a child."

The loss of San Luis was a turning point that caused Guevara to view the guerrillas' chances very critically. In his monthly summary for April, he pessimistically enumerated at least three major problems undermining his efforts. For the first time, he discussed in some detail the isolation of the band. He complained that the peasants were not responding and that there had been no enlistments.

According to Guevara, the arrests of Jules Regis Debray and the Argentine journalist, Ciro Bustos, that month further isolated the band from possible sources of foreign assistance.

Finally, Che opined that "the Americans will intervene here strongly." His basic strategy was to provoke US military intervention in Latin America, but it seems that he was unprepared to cope with such an intervention as early as April.

Leadership

During the following months, the band suffered a slow attrition while morale continued to plummet. Several more guerrillas were lost in skirmishes and others, including Guevara, were weakened and incapacitated by various ailments and injuries. By the end of July, Guevara was emphasizing only the "negative aspects" of the campaign and reiterated daily complaints about his asthma attacks. He was weak and ill, unable at times to carry his own knapsack.

The band of 22 was entirely on the defensive in remote and unplotted terrain while the Bolivian military was slowly increasing its effectiveness and encircling the guerrillas. In these circumstances, Guevara was facing increasingly serious problems, including chronic food shortages. Once, during a long period on reduced rations, members of the band suffered "fainting spells."

By the end of August, after almost ten months of attrition and debilitation, Guevara admitted that it had been "without a doubt the worst month yet." His illness, Che said, had "caused uncertainty in several others...and (was) reflected in our only encounter (with the army)." This was his only admission that his primacy was ever doubted.

In fact, however, Guevara had discipline problems almost from the outset. These resulted from the friction between the

Document 41 contd.

Bolivians and Cubans in the band, and from the lessening of morale as the hardships and setbacks increased. Che's leadership may also have been undermined by his own physical weakness and inability to engineer an effective offensive. In 11 months, Che had not been able to nurture his movement beyond the most preliminary stage of incipient insurgency.

The Guerrillas' Failure With the Peasants

In his handbook, *Guerrilla Warfare*, Guevara explained in detail how the guerrilla must win first the sympathy and trust and then the full collaboration of the rural peasants in order to sustain the struggle. In Bolivia, however, he found this goal impossible from the beginning because of the suspicions, fears, and torpor of the Indian peasants.

In April, Guevara complained that "the peasant base has not yet been developed although it would appear that through planned terror we shall keep some neutral." He admitted the extent of the guerrillas' isolation on 17 April, when he said that "of all the peasants we have seen, there is only one who appears to be cooperative, but with fear." In June, moreover, he warned that the Bolivian Army was "working on the peasants and we must be careful that they are not changed into a community of informers." Fearing betrayal by virtually everyone they encountered, Guevara and his followers wandered in isolation through the sparsely populated jungles.

The End of a Legend

During September and the first week of October, the guerrillas were constantly on the run, trapped in a maze of jungle arroyos. During the last weeks, when he must have known that his chances were bleak, Guevara continued to write in the same brief style with mystic hopes for victory. He made his last entry on 7 October, after exactly 11 months in Bolivia. He said the day "was spent in a pastoral setting," but apparently it was a peasant woman from that area who betrayed the guerrillas to the Bolivian forces. The woman had been bribed to keep the guerrillas' location secret, but Che confided in his last entry that he had "little hope she would keep her word."

Guevara was wounded and captured by Bolivian Rangers on 8 October and died the following day. On 16 October, Fidel Castro admitted Guevara's defeat. Two days later, he delivered a lengthy eulogy and declared a month of national mourning in Cuba.

In the diary, Che mentioned frequent communications with Castro. Though his transmitter was destroyed in January, Guevara communicated through couriers and was able to receive coded radio messages from Havana. There were no indications of differences between the two men.

Guevara, his lessons, and his legend were perhaps simultaneously stifled. Though Castro and other revolutionaries may insist that the struggle will endlessly continue in his name, they must now be having serious doubts about their prospects.

Document 41 contd.

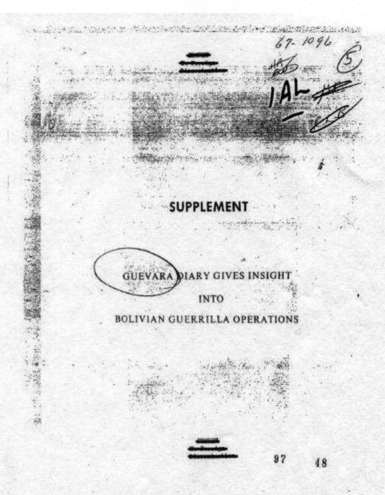

Document 42. DIA Intelligence Bulletin, Guevara Diary Gives Insight Into Bolivia Guerillas Operations (Dec. 15, 1967)

    This is the Dept. of Defense's intelligence Agency's evaluation (December 1967) of Che's Bolivian guerillas effort based upon their reading of his diary, taken from him after his capture. It concludes that Che's efforts were a "complete failure, without any saving aspects, of this first attempt to implement the Castro-Guevara-Debray theories on insurgency. . . ."

GUEVARA DIARY GIVES INSIGHT INTO
BOLIVIAN GUERRILLA OPERATIONS

"Che" Guevara's campaign diary -- captured when the guerrilla leader was killed in early October -- provides considerable information on the nature and scope of the Cuban-directed insurgent movement in southeast Bolivia and the reasons for its failure.

Guevara's death and the defeat of his guerrilla band in Bolivia was the most serious blow yet dealt to the Cuban doctrine of armed insurgency for Latin America, since Castro had apparently committed his "first team" to this effort. Of an estimated 12 Cubans killed in operations there, at least five have been identified as members of the Central Committee of the Cuban Communist Party (PCC); six held the rank of major, the highest in the Cuban armed forces and a number of them participated in guerrilla operations against the Batista forces.

The extent of Cuban involvement in the Bolivian operation indicates that Castro -- in conflict with the Soviets over Communist strategy in Latin America -- wanted a victory that would justify his advocacy of armed revolution. He either did not fear the possible implications of direct involvement or he was fully prepared to risk them.

The high-level Cuban participation also tends to support recent reports that the Bolivian operation was the first phase of a wider multinational offensive that was to be launched against other neighboring countries. To the Castro regime, Bolivia was probably ideally located for such an operation. Castro, however, apparently did not match his high-level commitment with a proper evaluation of the situation in Bolivia or with adequate planning and organization. "Che" Guevara's diary has revealed a basic weakness in Cuba's intelligence in that the whole operation was based on an overly optimistic estimate that as soon as operations commenced, a base could be established with peasant support. This was accompanied by an underestimation of the strength of the Bolivian armed forces and the

Document 42 contd.

BOLIVIAN LEADER GUIDO PEREDO AND TYPICAL TERRAIN
OF THE OPERATIONS ZONE. PEREDO IS STILL AT LARGE.

CUBAN AND DENSE VEGETATION WHICH PLAGUED
THE GUERRILLAS AS WELL AS THE PURSUING
BOLIVIAN ARMY

SECRET
15 DEC 67

Document 42 contd.

resolve of the Bolivian Government. Despite the early planning, the operation was generally an uncoordinated effort from the outset, and its inadequacies became apparent once operations began.

While guerrilla planning was apparently under way for some time in both Cuba and Bolivia, actual operations did not begin until "Che" and part of his Cuban cadre arrived at the Nancahuazu camp in November 1966. The next several months were devoted to training, recruitment, equipment caching, and area familiarization. During this period, "Che" led a reconnaissance patrol north of the Rio Grande; this was his first introduction to the hostile nature of the area. The guerrilla timetable apparently did not call for offensive action to begin until mid- or late-1967. Thus, when the army inadvertently discovered the guerrillas in March 1967, "Che's" force was still in its initial phase and was prematurely forced into action. Partly because of this, their sanctuary was uncovered and they were therefore forced to remain almost constantly on the move. This had upset "Che's" plans to establish a secure base of operations.

The guerrilla force, which at its highest point probably did not exceed 50 men, was composed of 17 Cubans, three Peruvians, Bolivians trained in Cuba, and urban militants. "Che" planned to use them as a cadre around which other guerrilla groups could be established. Some of the Bolivians apparently lacked the dedication and staying power of hard-core guerrillas and the diary reported resentment between the Bolivians and Cubans. Information obtained from Bolivian defectors enabled the army to uncover the guerrilla camp in March and to locate and eliminate the insurgents in October.

It was evident from the beginning that "Che" was in firm command of the guerrilla movement. This fact apparently cost him the support of the established pro-Soviet Bolivian Communist Party (PCB-S). According to the diary, PCB-S First Secretary Mario Monje visited the guerrilla camp in December 1966 and offered to join the movement provided he could assume the political-military leadership. "Che's" rejection of his bid probably severed any chances for a tie between the Party and the

Document 42 contd.

guerrillas. In fact, "Che" suspected that Monje had prevented some Cuban-trained Party members from joining the guerrillas. Regis Debray, the French guerrilla theoretician, also placed part of the blame for the guerrilla failure on the lack of support from the PCB-S.

One factor that weighed heavily against the guerrillas was the numerical strength of the army in the field. Even in the early stages of the operation, the army -- inferior in capabilities to the guerrillas -- was able to react with sufficient speed to thwart the insurgents' movements. The army was able to seal off most of the avenues of escape; this forced the guerrillas to be contantly on the move and drained their resources. Toward the end of the campaign, troops in the field probably numbered 2,000 as compared with the guerrilla's force of 30 - 40.

In addition to the role of the armed forces, the two other factors that contributed most significantly to the quick defeat of the guerrilla force were the nature of the guerrilla zone itself and the inability of the insurgents to win the support of the local populace.

Although the isolated southeastern region of Bolivia with its difficult terrain and dense jungle appeared ideal from a security standpoint, it is extremely inhospitable to man; it is disease-ridden and sparsely populated. Moreover, the operations zone was almost completely inaccessible to the main population centers in the Altiplano. On numerous occasions in his diary, "Che" bemoaned the almost total isolation of his force. Even the support apparatus in La Paz -- uncovered and smashed in September -- had trouble maintaining contact with guerrillas once they were forced out of the Nancahuazu base camp. "Che" also reported in the diary that he was unable to make contact with a small rearguard force that remained near the original camp. This group was eventually destroyed on 31 August by an army ambush after it had been isolated from the main force for over three months.

"Che" reported an acute lack of supplies -- including medicine for his disabling asthma -- chronic hunger,

Document 42 contd.

SECRET NO FOREIGN DISSEM

loss of bearings because of faulty maps, desertions by the Bolivians, debilitating illness, and a break-down in morale -- most of which occurred after June. Since actual contact between the armed forces and the guerrillas was minimal during this period, the dete-rioration of the insurgent force can be attributed in a large measure to the vast, remote, and hostile area which was selected for the operation.

Apparently, "Che" expected to exploit the reported latent antigovernment sentiment of the sparse peasant population in the operations zone. To this end, the guerrillas carried on something similar to a civil-action program. They provided medical care to the peasants and always paid them good prices for supplies. Despite these efforts, the peasants remained suspicious of foreigners and assumed a passive role throughout the entire campaign. Toward the latter stages of the campaign, peasant guides and informers assisted the army in tracking down and eliminating the force. A frustrated "Che" Guevara lamented several times in his diary over the inability of the guerrillas to recruit even one local peasant.

The complete failure, without any saving aspects, of this first attempt to implement the Castro-Guevara-Debray theories on insurgency will certainly cause a reevaluation in Havana. Whether the hard lessons of Bolivia will prevail against an almost sacred theory remains to be seen. (SECRET NO FOREIGN DISSEM)

SECRET NO FOREIGN DISSEM

Document 42 contd.

PAGE:0080

ALSO ON 13 JULY, THE REMAINS OF
LATIN AMERICAN REVOLUTIONARY HERO CHE GUEVARA, BURIED SINCE 1967
IN AN UNMARKED GRAVE IN RURAL BOLIVIA, WERE RETURNED TO CUBA.

3. (U) THE ABOVE WAS WRITTEN BY ANALYSTS OF DIA'S TERRORISM
WARNING DIVISION; QUESTIONS AND COMMENTS SHOULD BE DIRECTED TO
THIS OFFICE AT
PUBLICATION INFORMATION: THE DITSUM IS PUBLISHED DAILY MONDAY
THROUGH FRIDAY WITH INFORMATION CUT OFF AT 1500 EST. THE DITSUM
IS ALSO AVAILABLE ON INTELINK. IMMEDIATE TERRORIST THREAT

Document 43. DIA, Defense Intelligence Terrorism Summary, remains of Che returned to Cuba (July 15, 1997)

DEFENSE INTELLIGENCE AGENCY

WASHINGTON, D.C. 20340-5100

U-7,548-06/DAN-1A(FOIA)

APR 2 0 2007

Mr. Michael Ratner
124 Washington Place
New York, NY 10014

Dear Mr. Ratner:

This responds to your request under the Freedom of Information Act dated 18 April 1997.
Therein you requested records concerning Ernesto "Che" Guevara. A search of DIA's systems of
records located 101 documents. Of these, 52 have been referred to other government agencies
for their review and direct response to you as they did not originate with DIA.

Upon review, it has been determined that some portions of 39 documents are not releasable. The
portions withheld are exempt from release pursuant to 5 U.S.C. 552 (b)(1), (b)(2), and (b)(3),
Freedom of Information Act. Subsection (b)(1) applies to information properly classified under
the criteria provided by Executive Order 12958, as amended. Subsection (b)(2) applies to
information which pertains solely to the internal rules and practices of the agency. Subsection
(b)(3) applies to information specifically exempted by a statute establishing particular criteria for
withholding. The applicable statute is 10 U.S.C. Section 424. All reasonably segregable
portions are attached.

All substantive portions of the remaining 10 documents are not releasable. The withheld
portions are exempt from release pursuant to 5 U.S.C. 552 (b)(1), (b)(2), and (b)(3), Freedom of
Information Act. There are no reasonably segregable portions of this exempt material.

Please remit a check or money order in U.S. funds made payable to the Treasurer of the United
States in the amount of $35.40. Do not send cash. This fee is for reproduction cost for 336
pages at 15¢ per page with the first 100 pages free. To insure proper identification, please write
on your payment the case number assigned to your request, 0502-97.

You are advised that a requester may appeal, within 60 days, an initial decision to withhold a
record or part thereof. Should you wish to exercise this right, you may do so by referring to case
0502-97 and addressing your appeal to: Defense Intelligence Agency, ATTN: DAN-1(FOIA)
Washington, D.C. 20340-5100.

Sincerely,

Margaret A. Bestrain
Chief, Public Access Branch

39 Enclosures a/s

Document 43 contd.

ACKNOWLEDGMENTS

We would like to thank and acknowledge Joseph Craig, Editorial Director at Skyhorse Publishing, for recognizing the importance, both moral and political, of this book and for taking the initiative to republish it.

Thank you to everyone at OR Books, and especially to co-publisher Colin Robinson, for their work on this book. Thanks also to Pamela Lichty, Jed Brandt and Debby Smith for their assistance. We are indebted to Fox Butterfield Ryan, for obtaining many documents and writing the excellent study "The Fall of Che Guevara" and to Peter Kornbluh of the National Security Archives for obtaining and interpreting many of the documents as well. We thank a number of our Cuban comrades who met and spoke with us in Havana. They are: Alieda March, Che's widow; Harry "Pombo" Villegas, now a general in the Cuban army who fought with Che in the Cuban revolution, in the Congo, and in Bolivia; Ulises Estrada, a key organizer of Che Guevara's guerilla mission to Bolivia; Mirta Munoz, a veteran of the Cuban Revolution and representative of Ocean Press who helped us so much in Havana; Adys Cupull and Froilan Gonzalez, the Cuban authors of *A Brave Man,* for meeting with us and giving us their fine chronology of Che's life. Finally, thank you to Deb Schnookal of that invaluable resource Ocean Press, whose original idea it was to produce this book.

ABOUT THE AUTHORS

Michael Ratner (1943–2016) was President of the Center for Constitutional Rights (CCR), a non-profit human-rights litigation organization. He and CCR were co-counsel in representing Guantanamo Bay detainees in the United States Supreme Court. His leadership in the arena of human rights strengthened the role of the international rule of law to promote justice and oppose armed aggression. He was President of the European Center for Constitutional and Human Rights (ECCHR), an independent, non-profit organization dedicated seeking redress for those whose human rights have been egregiously violated. He was the author or co-author of many books and articles, including *Hell No, Your Right to Dissent in Twenty-First Century America, The Trial of Donald Rumsfeld: A Prosecution by Book, Against War with Iraq, Guantanamo: What the World Should Know* and the textbook, *International Human Rights Litigation in U. S. Courts.* He taught law at Yale and Columbia Law Schools. He was the co-host of the popular radio program *Law and Disorder* and blogged at www.justleft.org. The recipient of many honors, he was named in The National Law Journal's list of "100 of the Most Influential Lawyers in America."

Michael Steven Smith has testified on human-rights issues before committees of the United Nations and the U.S. Congress. He is a member of the board of The Center for Constitutional Rights. He edited, with Michael Ratner, a collection of documents *Che Guevara and the FBI: The U.S. Political Police Dossier on the Latin American Revolutionary* and has written *Notebook of a Sixties Lawyer: An Unrepentant Memoir* and *Lawyers You'll Like: Putting Human Rights Before Property Rights.* He co-edited *The Emerging Police State* by William M. Kunstler with Sarah Kunstler and Karen Kunstler Goldman. He is co-host of the WBAI radio show *Law and Disorder* (on the net at lawanddisorder.org) with Heidi Boghosian (and previously with Michael Ratner) and has the blog michaelstevensmith.com. He practices law in New York City, where he lives with his wife Debby and talking parrot Charlie Parker.

INDEX